PLANTATION HOMES OF THE TECHE COUNTRY

Plantation Homes
of the
Teche Country

by PAUL F. STAHLS JR.
photography by Leonard Hingle

PELICAN PUBLISHING COMPANY GRETNA 1985

Library of Congress Cataloging in Publication Data

Stahls, Paul F.
    Plantation homes of the Teche country.

    Includes index.
    1. Historic buildings--Louisiana--Teche Bayou--
Guide-books. 2. Teche Bayou--Description and travel--
Guide-books. 3. Plantations--Louisiana--Teche Bayou--
Guide-books. I. Hingle, Leonard. II. Title.
F377.T4S72   917.63'04'6   78-24283
ISBN 0-88289-205-3

First printing, 1979
Second printing, 1985

Manufactured in the United States of America

Published by Pelican Publishing Company, Inc.
1101 Monroe Street, Gretna, Louisiana 70053
Designed by Mike Burton

Frontispiece: *The columns, latticework and gallery stairway of Shadows-on-the-Teche in New Iberia.*

To Peggy, for waiting

Acknowledgments

Many have contributed time and knowledge to this volume, but no one has had to "live" the book (or endure it) more than my wife, Peggy. Thank you for your suggestions and contributions, but most of all for pretending not to enjoy my frequent disappearances.

My wonderful Peggy Goudeau is still typing, and I must again thank the three newspapers that fed me in my student years by using portions of this book (and of the preceding volume, *Plantation Homes of the Lafourche Country*) in the form of a weekly column—the Lafourche (Thibodaux) *Daily Comet*, the Houma *Daily Courier*, and the Morgan City *Daily Review*.

I speak for many Louisianians when I thank Mr. Morris Raphael of New Iberia for giving us *The Battle in the Bayou Country* (Harlo Press, 1975). That book is our most understandable account of the Bayou Country campaign, and it is cited often in this one.

I am grateful to the Louisiana Department of Culture, Recreation and Tourism, Division of Archaeology and Historic Preservation for making available its files on the Teche Country structures that are listed on the National Register of Historic Places.

The owners of the Adrien Persac paintings that appear in the book deserve special recognition for allowing them to be photographed and shared with all of us. These are Mrs. Edward J. Gilly of New Orleans, the National Trust for Historic Preservation, Mr. Arthur Lemann, Jr. of Palo Alto Plantation near Donaldsonville, Mr. Felix Kuntz of New Orleans (deceased), and Mr. and Mrs. Frederick Nehrbass of Lafayette.

Finally, I must extend a special thank you to those who gladly went beyond the call of duty in providing information on the homes of their areas—Mrs. Florence Blackburn of Franklin, Mr. Frank R. Duke of Jeanerette, Mrs. Virginia Kyle Hine of New Iberia, Mr. James Acres and Mrs. Leona Martin Guirard of St. Martinville, Mr. C. Kenneth Deshotel of Opelousas, Mrs. Chloe Mills of the Grand Coteau area, Mrs. Euna Evans of Abbeville, and Mrs. Lloyd Barras of Lake Charles.

Contents

Oaklawn's old butterhouse is nestled between some of the mighty oaks from which the manor takes its name.

PLANTATION HOMES OF THE TECHE COUNTRY

One of the finest of Albania's many plaster medallions and crystal chandeliers may be found in the large dining room.

Introduction

A giant snake, according to Indian legend, slithered across south-central Louisiana one day, sending every camp into near panic with his huge fangs and hissing noises. Thousands of braves filled his sides with arrows. The snake writhed in agony for days and then lay stunned, whereupon the Indians beat him to death with clubs. When his body had turned to dust and blown away, the natives found that his writhing had hollowed out a long, twisting trench in the earth, which soon filled with water. They called the new waterway "Tenche," meaning "snake." French settlers later softened the name to "Teche."[1]

In ancient times Bayou Teche was the main channel of the Mississippi River itself. Today it borders the Atchafalaya Basin, and the Teche Ridge is the western boundary of the great Mississippi River floodplain. In 1760 the first permanent settlement on the Teche was established at what is now St. Martinville. The Acadians, recently exiled from today's Nova Scotia, arrived in 1766. The French Revolution and the slave revolts in the West Indies brought many displaced French aristocrats to the area, and after 1803 came the Americans.

Up and down the Teche today can be seen the Creole raised cottages of the French-Spanish period of settlement, the Creole-Caribbean cabins (now called "Cajun cabins") that were adopted by the Acadian exiles, and the Greek Revival mansions of the American period. Visitors also see mile upon mile of the beautiful natural landscaping for which Bayou Teche is famous, with its rows of giant oaks, its sugarcane, magnolias, orange trees, and flowers of every description. Henry Wadsworth Longfellow described it thus:

> Beautiful is the land, with its prairies
>   and forests of fruit-trees;
> Under the feet a garden of flowers
>   and the bluest of heavens
> Bending above, and resting its dome
>   on the walls of the forest.
> They who dwell there have named it
>   the Eden of Louisiana!

We will begin our tour near Morgan City and visit the historic homes and buildings in and between Patterson, Centerville, Franklin, Jeanerette, Patoutville, New Iberia, St. Martinville, and Breaux Bridge. Charles Gilbert Stahls, in his novel *Grand Bouquet* about Louisiana in the socially turbulent days after World War II, had this to say about the highway we will follow. It "traverses an area that is guaranteed to delight the eye of any but the most indifferent traveler. It winds through the Teche, or Evangeline, region, made famous by Longfellow's epic poem, through tiny villages and carefree, somnolent towns, their broad main streets bordered by spreading live oaks festooned with Spanish moss. . . . Flower lovers find themselves in a floral paradise, for blossoms indigenous to temperate, semitropical, subtropical and even tropical climes abound on all sides."[2]

We will also visit the famous tropical gardens of Avery Island and Jefferson Island and such "new" historical attractions as Heritage Village in Loreauville, Acadian Village in Lafayette, and Heritage Farm in Branch. Finally, we will see the antebellum homes that lie to the south and west of Bayou Teche.

This book is the second in a series on the historic homes and buildings of Louisiana, the first of which was *Plantation Homes of the Lafourche Country*. A proposed third volume, *Plantation Homes of the Cotton Country*, will begin in Opelousas and cover the many fine old homes of North Louisiana.

Attached by a sheltered carriage drive to Shadowlawn's rear galleries is a rear wing that is actually much older than the larger front portion of the mansion. The little cottage was already standing when Simeon Smith purchased the property in 1833, and he lived in it until the more spacious section was complete.

Bayou Teche

From Morgan City, cross the Atchafalaya River (Berwick Bay) on U.S. 90. From the first Berwick Exit it is 4.5 miles farther on U.S. 90 to an exit onto Highway 182 (at a point where Highway 182 is parallel to U.S. 90). Exit, turn left on Highway 182, and drive 0.1 mile around a sharp right curve to the home called Idlewild.

IDLEWILD

Idlewild (private) is set on the west bank of the Lower Atchafalaya, now controlled by locks, which runs into Berwick Bay at Berwick and Morgan City. The single gallery of this two-story home is lined by six fluted Doric columns, and a dentil course adorns the entablature. A set of balconies, upper and lower, can be seen on each side of the house, and each set is supported by octagonal columns.

A sugar planter named Georges Haydel began the construction of Idlewild in 1850. The home, built of cypress, pine, and brick, was completed in 1854, and Haydel presented it immediately or soon afterward to his daughter, a Mrs. Briant. It was purchased shortly after the War Between the States by Captain I. D. Seyburn of the U.S. Navy, who had commanded one of the ships in Admiral Farragut's blockade fleet. The captain's grandson, Edward R. Seyburn, restored the home in 1964.

All the woodwork of Idlewild is original, from the floors to the hand-planed doors, as well as many of the windowpanes. The French doors that open onto the front and rear galleries are unusual. The shutters open to reveal ordinary windows above and small (perhaps two-foot-high) doors below. With the windows open and the small doors closed, one has windows. With the windows and the tiny doors open, doorways are created.

Pine lumber was brought from the East Coast for the floors and walls. Cypress, however, was used for the exterior and for all millwork. The ironwork of the vents around the base of the house, and of the balustrades of the gallery and balconies, is of a handsome and unusual design. The octagonal columns of the balconies are repeated on the rear gallery, which overlooks the Lower Atchafalaya.

Drive 5.4 miles farther along Highway 182, through the town of Patterson, to Calumet—your first stop on Bayou Teche. The bayou runs into the Lower Atchafalaya at a point between Idlewild and Calumet that cannot be seen from the highway.

BATTLE OF BISLAND

General "Spoons" Butler in New Orleans had dispatched General Godfrey Weitzel, late in 1862, to eliminate the Confederate forces of General Richard Taylor (son of President Zachary Taylor and brother-in-law of President Jefferson Davis) in the Bayou Country, and possibly to neutralize certain Texas cities that were being used as Confederate supply points. (Occupation would also prevent a Texas alliance with Mexico, which, rumor had it, was in the offing.) Weitzel's progress through the Lafourche country (down Bayou Lafourche from Donaldsonville and then overland to the west) had been constantly hampered by Confederate rearguard action and major skirmishes, but by November four Federal gunboats and troops had occupied Brashear (Morgan) City and Berwick Bay, and the Confederates had retreated a short distance up Bayou Teche.

Confederate General Alfred Mouton (from Lafayette) had begun constructing Fort Bisland, at a point on the bayou just above Patterson, and Captain E. W. Fuller had been sent with the gunboat Cotton to delay Federal gunboats long enough for Mouton to complete his fortifications. On November 3, the Cotton successfully fought off the Calhoun, Estrella, Kinsman, and Diana; and Fuller also defeated the Calhoun and Estrella in a return engagement on November 5.

(The Diana was miraculously captured by the Confederates in late March, 1863.)

On November 8, 1862, President Lincoln named Nathaniel P. Banks to replace Butler as commander of the Department of the Gulf. Banks arrived in Morgan City on April 8, 1863, with eighteen thousand additional troops and a plan. He would send his boats ladened with troops up the Atchafalaya and through Grand Lake to the Teche, above the forces of Mouton and Taylor at Bisland and Franklin. His main force would move up the Teche, and the Confederates would be trapped and crushed.

Banks and the main body crossed Berwick Bay on April 12 and, with the gunboats on their way through Grand Lake, proceeded up the bayou. Taylor joined Mouton at Bisland, and a small force was sent to prevent or delay the Union landing above Franklin. Banks arrived at Bisland at 5 p.m. and was immediately penned down by heavy fire from the ground

Idlewild, built in 1850, stands on the Lower Atchafalaya near Patterson.

Calumet, on beautiful Bayou Teche. History has occurred on its very lawn, from Civil War battles to pioneer aviation.

and from the Diana. *At sunset, Banks withdrew.*[3] *Banks launched two unsuccessful charges on the morning of April 13. The* Diana, *crippled by artillery fire, was forced to withdraw for repairs.*

Taylor received word late in the day that the Union troops from Grand Lake had landed on the Teche above Franklin. The Confederates abandoned Bisland under cover of darkness, arriving in Franklin about 2 a.m. on April 14. They deployed above the town in the cane fields at a great loop in Bayou Teche called Irish Bend.

CALUMET

Calumet (private) was constructed in the 1840s or 1850s, but the first records show its being purchased some time later by Daniel Thompson. The Chicago industrialist had come to the South for reasons of health, and he assembled many small tracts into a huge sugar plantation.

This is a two-story cottage with eight square columns across its eighty-six-foot gallery. The Bayou Room was added to the rear of the home in 1950, and around three sides of the room runs a shallow porch with columns identical to those of the gallery. Beneath a giant magnolia beside the home stands a large weatherboarded house, formerly a slave dwelling, which was moved from another location on the plantation to serve as a guest house.

The oldest section of Calumet includes four rooms downstairs and two upstairs. These rooms can be detected today by tapping the walls, which are thick and constructed of bricks between wall studs. Today's foyer, drawing room, dining room, and music room, as well as the rooms directly above, are included in this original section.

The Fortuné drapery of the drawing room and dining room is of hand-painted silk, and stunning mantels of white marble enhance the fireplaces of these two rooms. In the music room is a Playell piano which dates to 1835. A wide transomed passageway leads from the music room to the Bayou Room, aptly named, where a huge picture window offers a panorama of oaks, pecan trees, and camellias on the gently sloping lawn that leads down to beautiful Bayou Teche.

In a side hallway hang three sketches done by Daniel Thompson in 1870—one of the home, one of the home and yard, and one of the entire plantation. A stairway leads from this hall to the rooms above.

Just across the highway from Calumet is the Williams Memorial Airport, where Harry P. Williams (born in Patterson) and James R. Wedell operated the Wedell-Williams Air Service from 1929 to 1936. During this time they designed and built "some of the fastest land-based airplanes of their time." They set many records and won national recognition, receiving such awards as the Bendix and Thompson trophies. The Louisiana Aviation Museum is now located at the old airstrip.

Williams married silent-screen star Marguerite Clark, and at least one movie, entitled (provocatively) *Louisiana Hussy*, was filmed at Calumet. Williams had purchased the home in 1935 and was in the process of restoring it when he lost his life the next year.

Drive 1.5 miles farther along Highway 182, and turn right on U.S. 90. Drive 1.4 miles, turn right on Highway 182, and drive 1.7 miles to a small raised cottage, set far back from the highway on the right.

RAISED COTTAGE

This house is well over one hundred years old, as can be determined by its pegged cypress construction. Six colonettes and a balustrade enclose the single gallery, which is served by a transomed door and two shuttered windows. In the yard is an old plantation bell.

Drive 3.5 miles farther along Highway 182 to the Centerville Presbyterian Church, on the left.

Construction of Centerville's Presbyterian church was delayed by the war until 1876.

CENTERVILLE

The little town of Centerville was so named because it was once the "center," the shipping point, for this sugar-rich section of the Teche country.

Centerville Presbyterian Church

Land for Centerville's Presbyterian church was acquired in 1860 by a congregation which had been formed only shortly before. The War Between the States interrupted the plans for construction, however, and it was not until 1876 that the reorganized congregation was able to begin work. The building was dedicated in 1878.

Black-shuttered windows line this simple, weatherboarded structure. A spire, square and also of weatherboards, rises from the large entrance. The mahogany pulpit inside is said to be original to the church.

Shakespeare Allen House

Just past the Presbyterian church, on the left, is a large white home with four fluted Corinthian columns. The facade consists of two galleries and a pediment, which is ornamented with a dentil course. The back of the Shakespeare Allen House (private) is identical to the front.

This home was constructed by Simeon Smith prior to 1854. Later, Thomas David Hine, who purchased it in 1861, sold it to David Berwick. Then came Dr. Shakespeare Allen. The home was inherited by Allen's daughters, one of whom bought her sisters' shares. She sold the structure to the Woodmen of the World (Pecan Camp Number 41) in 1908, but it has since returned to private ownership.

This order of ownership may not be perfectly correct as stated. Some say that Shakespeare Allen's wife was the daughter of Simeon Smith, and others say she was the daughter of David Berwick (an uncertainty of history, not a rumor of scandal). In any event, either Smith built or

Berwick bought the home for Mrs. Allen, and Allen either preceded or followed Berwick in ownership. Simeon Smith was also the builder of Shadowlawn in Franklin.

The Shakespeare Allen House is furnished beautifully with tapestry from the period of construction. Some of the fine antiques include marbled dressers and an unusual brass halftester bed.

Vetter House

Next door to the Shakespeare Allen House stands an antebellum home called the Vetter House (private). Four stately, square columns front the wide, pedimented portico. The second-floor gallery is enclosed by a balustrade of a crossed-diamond design. Much of the land between Centerville and Franklin was included in the original Spanish land grant to Louis Georges de Maret, and his granddaughter, Mrs. Elizabeth Hawkins, was once the owner of the Vetter House.

Old Kennedy Hotel

Directly across Highway 182 from the Vetter House stands the Old Kennedy Hotel, which now serves as a branch of the Commercial Bank and Trust Company of Franklin. The builder is unknown, but it is certain that the building was constructed prior to 1855. This structure, with its large square columns and gable roof, was owned from 1870 to 1901 by a man named Thomas Kennedy. It served during those years as a hotel as well as his home.

Inside are a beautiful stairway, plaster medallions, and woodwork that is ornamented in the ancient art of *faux bois* ("false wood"—one wood painted to resemble another). The old hotel has received restoration work at the hands of the bank.

From the Old Kennedy Hotel it is 0.6 mile farther along Highway 182 to the home now called Bocage.

BOCAGE

This home (private) was first called Oak Bluff,

The Shakespeare Allen house, built prior to 1854.

The Vetter house faces Highway 90 in the heart of Centerville.

The old Kennedy Hotel, constructed prior to 1855. Now a bank, this old hotel was once the center of social activity in Centerville.

for it stood on an oak-shaded mound on the east bank of Bayou Teche's Irish Bend near Franklin. Mr. and Mrs. Edward H. Sutter had the huge house moved seven miles down the bayou by barge to its present location in 1969, and they renamed it Bocage. The present owner (1978), Mrs. Fairfax Foster Sutter, is the great-granddaughter of Governor Murphy J. Foster, whose old home, Dixie, is nearby. Bocage now stands on land that was part of the large tract granted to Louis Georges de Maret by the Spanish government, and Mrs. Sutter is a fifth-generation descendant of de Maret.

The pedimented portico of Bocage is fronted by four massive square columns. The pediment is ornamented by a small vented window and a dentil course, and the two galleries are enclosed by attractive wooden balustrades. The two small

Bocage, once called Oak Bluff. The mansion was built in 1846 and moved by barge seven miles down Bayou Teche to its present setting.

side wings in the rear of the home are not original to the structure, but they repeat the design of the facade in a modified form.

Much of the furniture of Bocage came from The Cottage, once owned by Mrs. Sutter's family, whose beautiful ruins still stand on the east bank of the Mississippi below Baton Rouge. Items of particular interest are the doors, several of which feature *faux bois* ornamentation, mantels and crystal chandeliers from Ireland and Scotland, the Henry Clay desk used by the statesman on a visit to The Cottage, a clock from The Cottage that dates to 1753, the Governor Johnson bed with its acanthus-leaf carving, and the portraits of Governor and Mrs. Murphy J. Foster.[4]

A sugar plantation, mill, and commissary stood at the original site of Oak Bluff as early as 1826. David Bell purchased the fifteen hundred acres in 1846, and it is believed that he built the home that same year. He sold the house and land to Mrs. Zeide Foster (widow of Levi Foster) and her son, Thomas Jefferson Foster (Mrs. Sutter's great-grandfather).

Though several houses have been moved by barge on Bayou Teche, Bocage is said to be the largest. It was handled by Roy Berard and Sons, who performed the task so perfectly that not one of the original windowpanes of the home was broken.

Drive 0.9 mile farther along Highway 182 to an old home on the left called Susie.

SUSIE

This square, yellow frame house (private) is crowned by a hipped roof. Each of the two front galleries is fronted by six small square columns and a wooden balustrade. The two galleries on the rear are lined with six square two-story columns. A small stairway rises from the lower rear gallery to the upper. Susie was restored in 1970 by the Sutters of Bocage. The home was constructed around 1852 by one Royal Harris, on land that had been part of the original de Maret land grant. Mrs. Harris's grave may still be seen in the side yard.

From Susie, drive 0.6 mile up Highway 90 (182) to the beautiful little plantation house called Frances.

FRANCES

This raised cottage was built in 1820 on land that had been granted to Marc Navarro by the Spanish government and purchased by Louis Georges de Maret to add to his own grant, which already amounted to a small kingdom. The home remained in the de Maret family until 1876, when Mrs. Elizabeth de Maret Hawkins moved to the Vetter House in Centerville. In 1879 Frances was purchased by Louis Kramer, and it was he who gave the home its name, in honor of his daughter.

In recent years the little house has served as the home for overseers of the plantation on

Frances, built in 1820, now houses a gifts and antiques shop.

which it stands. In 1963, however, it was restored by Mrs. Fairfax Sutter of Bocage and her cousin, Mrs. Winifred Lucas of Baton Rouge, to house a gift and antique shop (which is, for all practical purposes, a museum of beautiful pieces of antique furniture, crystal, and silver). The shop is open Tuesday through Saturday from 9:00 a.m. to 5:00 p.m., and browsers are welcome.

Four square columns of white brick support the upper gallery of Frances, while four colonettes support the roof. The white balustrade, and two doors and four windows with their original shutters and panes, complete the facade. The rear gallery of Frances, now enclosed in glass, overlooks the oak-shaded backyard which leads down to the tranquil Teche. The white, hand-carved mantels inside the shop should be noticed above all else. On the sides of the house stand a green-latticed cistern and two outbuildings brought from other plantations, where they had once served as slave quarters.

From Frances it is 0.9 mile to the plantation home called Alice C.

ALICE C.

The old home called Alice C. (private) now serves as the office building for Alice C. Plantations. Six square columns and a white balustrade

Alice C., circa 1846. The old plantation home now serves as the office building of Alice C. Plantations.

line each of the two galleries of Alice C., and a dentil course adorns the entablature. Short, straight stairways lead to the center and to one side of the lower gallery. The house is said to have been built by Jotham Bedell, who was owner of the property from 1846 to 1859. The lines of the mantels and of the facings of doors and windows throughout the house are simple and beautiful. A long and lovely mahogany stairway graces the hallway.

It is 0.8 mile farther along Highway 90 (182) to Dixie.

DIXIE

Dixie (private) is a two-story house, constructed entirely of cypress. Four large square columns line its pedimented portico. The green trim of the door facings, louvered shutters, and balustrades adds attractive outlining to the home. The porticoes are now screened, awning has been added, and wings were added to the sides and rear of the home some years ago.

Dixie was built in 1850 or 1851 by the Richard A. Wilkins family. It was purchased in 1886 by Murphy J. Foster, a young lawyer during the hard years of Reconstruction. He served in the Louisiana Senate from 1880 to 1892, and it was in 1892 that he was elected thirty-first governor of Louisiana. His second term ended in 1900, and he served as a U.S. senator from 1901 to 1912. He was the last governor to serve two consecutive terms in Louisiana until John McKeithen renewed the practice in 1968. During his governorship, Foster led the opposition to the Louisiana Lottery, initiated direct primary election laws, and proclaimed the first Louisiana Thanksgiving on November 22, 1892. Dixie is now (1978) the home of Mrs. Paul W. Trowbridge, daughter of Governor Foster.

It is 0.4 mile from Dixie to Arlington (on the right) on the outskirts of the town of Franklin.

ARLINGTON

A circular drive leads from a handsome iron fence to the three-story home called Arlington (private). This mansion was built in the 1850s, probably by Euphrazie Carlin, son of Honoré

Carlin of an old and prominent Bayou Teche family. The home was restored in 1904 by J. Soule Martel, in 1935 by Clarence Lawless, and again in 1965 by the Carl Bauers.

Arlington is fronted by a pedimented portico featuring elaborate wrought-iron balustrades and four fluted Corinthian columns. The pediment is ornamented with a dentil course and a star-burst medallion. The bayou side of Arlington is identical to the front, although the rear galleries have been enclosed with glass. Smaller porticoes with one-story Corinthians can be seen on either side of the old structure.

The cornices throughout Arlington, redone in wood by the Bauers from the fragments of the old plaster cornices, are greatly projected and form the final perfect detail of the gigantic rooms. The plaster medallions (originals) are different in every room, and from these hang a variety of chandeliers.

Crossing hallways divide the rooms of the lower floor. From the hall in the right wing rises a handsome, curved stairway. The ornate white mantels of the two parlors are noteworthy. The marble mantel of the library is original, and the shelving here is of remilled cypress from an ancient building that was razed near Patterson.

FRANKLIN

Franklin was founded by an Englishman named Alexander Lewis and named for Poor Richard. It was in 1814 that Lewis purchased the already subdivided property and donated land for a courthouse and other parish buildings. (The settlement, previously called Carlin, had been named parish seat when St. Mary Parish was created in 1811.) Lewis donated property for a school in 1816 and a church in 1817.[5]

St. Mary is rich in sugarcane, corn, rice, beef cattle, oil, gas, forestry (hardwood and cypress), fur, shells (for lime and construction), and carbon black (for rubber, paint, ink, paper, and chemicals). The Chittimacha Indians, who lived along Grand Lake, were the first inhabitants of the area, at least as far back as history records. White men began arriving around 1765 and

Arlington, built in the 1850s. Corinthian columns grace the porticoes of all four sides of the old home.

settled along Bayous Boeuf and Teche. A portion of the old County of Attakapas became St. Martin Parish, and St. Mary was carved out of St. Martin in 1811. The parish has roughly 600 miles of navigable waterways.

Franklin, incorporated in 1830, is the town that Lyle Saxon called "one of the prettiest of Louisiana towns, all cool and green and white, with old homes standing back on smooth green lawns, amid clumps of banana trees and oleanders."[6] And Franklin is even more beautiful now than it was in Saxon's day—the trees are larger, the lawns are shadier, and the houses have had another half-century in which to acquire the mellow beauty that time alone can bestow.

Highway 90 (182) becomes East Main Street in Franklin, a boulevard that extends several blocks to the courthouse square. It is probably the most beautiful city street in Louisiana. The neutral ground is lined with attractive lampposts that were erected in 1908, and antebellum homes adorn both sides of the street. (The design of the lampposts allows them to be turned ninety degrees to facilitate the passing of sugarcane trucks during the grinding season.)

At 93 East Main Street in Franklin, on the southwest corner of Foster and East Main, stands the home called Shady Retreat.

The home at 114 East Main Street in Franklin was constructed in the 1850s.

Shady Retreat

The four great Corinthian columns of Shady Retreat (private) support a large pediment and front the two screened galleries, which are enclosed by wrought-iron balustrades. The home was built in 1854 by John Murphy for his daughter, Mrs. Thomas J. Foster. It was originally of the raised-cottage type of architecture. W. Prescott Foster, grandson of the builder and son of Governor Murphy J. Foster, enlarged the building to two and one-half stories and created the present facade in the 1930s. Shady Retreat is now (1978) owned by Mrs. W. P. Foster.

One block past Shady Retreat, on the right, is the home numbered 114 East Main Street.

114 East Main Street

Framed by giant oaks, the home at 114 East Main Street (private) in Franklin was constructed in the 1850s by an Englishman named Thomas Smardon. The two galleries and the pediment are supported by four towering square columns. The balustrade on the upper gallery is of white wood, ornately designed and trimmed in green.

Continue to the Palfrey House (on the right) at 200 East Main Street.

The Palfrey House, probably built in 1851.

Palfrey House

The Palfrey House (private) is fronted by a large pediment and four fluted, hand-carved Corinthian columns. Black ironwork encloses the screened upper gallery, and the facade is duplicated on the bayou side of the home. The house stands on land that was cultivated as early as 1840 by the Sterling family. This family sold the land in 1842 to Simon C. Mathison, who operated a gristmill on the property. Two fifteen-hundred-pound millstones of limestone may still be seen on the grounds.

Joshua Baker and his son Anthony W. Baker bought the land in 1851, and it is likely that the house was built by them that same year. Joshua Baker was born in 1799 in Mason County, Kentucky, and he moved with his family in 1811 to property that is now part of Oaklawn Plantation. He graduated from West Point in 1819, passed the bar in Kentucky in 1822, and returned to Louisiana to practice law. He was appointed judge of St. Mary Parish in 1829. Though he was a conservative Democrat, he opposed secession, and he was named governor of Louisiana in 1868 by the Union military authorities of the Department of the Gulf. Baker was replaced later in 1868 by Henry Clay Warmoth.

Shortly after 1851 the Palfrey House became

The John O'Niell house was built by the father of Governor Murphy Foster.

the home of Joshua Baker's son-in-law, Charlie Palfrey, who occupied it until 1869. The home served as a young ladies' boarding school during the Reconstruction years, but it was returned to Palfrey ownership in 1892 when it was purchased by Mrs. Willie Palfrey.[7] It is now (1978) the home of Mr. David H. Stiel, Jr. and his wife, the former Miss Patricia Palfrey.

Directly across East Main from the Palfrey House is the John O'Niell House, numbered 201.

John O'Niell House

The John O'Niell House (private) was built in 1851 by Thomas J. Foster, father of Governor Murphy J. Foster. Thomas Foster sold the home in 1854 when he married and moved to Shady Retreat. The house was purchased in 1873 by Franklin mayor Wilson McKerall, Jr., who was followed in office, in name, and in the home by Mayor Wilson McKerall III. He sold the home in 1895 to his son-in-law, Mayor John O'Niell.

The facade of the John O'Niell House includes four one-story square columns, a balustrade of white wood trimmed in green, louvered shutters on the windows, and two huge dormers above.

Continue to the Gates House (on the left) at 205 East Main.

Gates House

The Gates House (private) is topped by a hipped roof and an attractive belvedere. The main gallery and two short side galleries are lined with eight one-story, fluted Corinthian columns. The house stands on high foundations of green brick, and the gallery's balustrade of crossed-diamond design is repeated on the belvedere. The windows are ornamented by louvered shutters and attractive facings.

The home was constructed between 1851 and 1858 by Alfred Gates, and it was later the home of his daughter, Mrs. Susan Cornelia Palfrey. Next came Matthew Bells, who stayed for fifty years before it was purchased in 1965 by Mrs. R. E. Brumby, great-granddaughter of Alfred Gates.

Continue to the Porter Allen House (on the left) at 301 East Main Street.

Porter Allen House

The Porter Allen House (private) was built between 1845 and 1850 by William Porter Allen (building contractor and first mayor of Franklin) for Simon C. Mathison. It was later purchased by Judge A. C. Allen, son of Porter Allen and also a Franklin mayor. The home

The Gates house, and one of the pretty old lampposts of Franklin's beautiful East Main Street. The lamps are turned sideways in grinding season to allow easier passage for the sugar cane trucks.

The Porter Allen house, built by the first mayor of Franklin.

remained in the Allen family until 1972. The Allen House is surrounded by magnolias, large oaks, and much foliage. Four square columns support both galleries and the simple pediment.

Continue to the Old Hine House (on the left) at 305 East Main.

Old Hine House

Four heavy, fluted Corinthian columns front the weatherboarded Old Hine House, which is now called The Columns (private). Black iron grillwork encloses a long balcony above the gallery. An arched recess leads to the doorway, which is ornamented by a fanlight and two engaged Corinthian miniatures. Originally built at the location of today's post office, the house was taken down in 1910 and reassembled at its present address by George Palfrey.

East Main Street leads a short distance from the Old Hine House to the courthouse square.

Courthouse Square

The old St. Mary Parish Courthouse was destroyed in recent years and replaced by the nondescript structure that stands here today. Facing Main Street in front of the building are two statues. One is of Donelson Caffery, a sugar planter, lawyer, Confederate soldier, and U.S. senator (1892–1901). Behind this is a statue that stands in tribute to the Confederate soldiers of

St. Mary Parish, who "fought for the honor of their state and country."

Just behind the courthouse on the near bank of Bayou Teche, nearly buried, is a boiler from the gunboat *Diana*. The *Diana* was captured from and used against Union forces in the Battles of Bisland and Irish Bend, and it was scuttled here on April 14, 1863, to prevent its recapture.

A few blocks past the courthouse square, at 906 West Main Street (on the right), stands Shadowlawn.

Above left: The old Hine house. Four mighty Corinthians support the hipped roof.

Above right: On the bank of Bayou Teche, behind the courthouse building in Franklin, is a boiler from the gunboat Diana, *nearly buried. The* Diana *participated in the battles of Bisland and Irish Bend.*

Shadowlawn

The front steps of Shadowlawn (private) extend the entire length of the lower gallery, which is set perhaps two feet off the ground. From this gallery rise six fluted Corinthian columns. These support the upper gallery and the entablature, which is ornamented with a dentil course. Large doorways and windows with louvered shutters complete the facade. A rear section of the home is connected by a carriage drive beneath an upper gallery, which is supported by more of the giant Corinthians. A small side gallery on the rear section is lined with one-story Corinthian columns.

Shadowlawn was constructed of black pine from New York and of cypress beams. The bricks are of clay, and the plaster is of sand and horsehair. The builder was Simeon Smith, who was born in Connecticut in 1796. He worked with his father in shipping sugar and cotton to

Shadowlawn, at 906 West Main Street, is one of Franklin's most beautiful homes.

the Northern states and returning with merchandise for the Southern states. In 1830 Smith left the family home in Memphis to live in Louisiana. In 1833 he told his parents by letter (still in the possession of the family) that he had found the spot where he wished to build his home. The rear section of Shadowlawn was already standing in 1833, and he lived there during the construction of the section which is visible from Main Street. Smith died of yellow fever in 1853, and Shadowlawn is now (1978) owned by his great-granddaughter, Mrs. T. D. Snowden of Memphis and Franklin.

Family portraits hang in the forty-five-foot hallway. The mahogany stairway here is exquisite, and the old curved servants stair still rises from the back of the hall. The ceilings of Shadowlawn are about fifteen feet high. The door facings throughout the home are all slightly different, though each is elegant and simple. The porcelain knobs and the keys and covered keyholes are all original. In the drawing room are the original valances and tiebacks, as well as portraits of Simeon Smith, his mother, and his father.

The tremendous Smith Oak on the bayou side of the home was one of the earliest members of the Louisiana Live Oak Society. Standing on the mansion's upper gallery beside the magnificent Corinthian capitals of the columns, one can see the old brick walk that leads beneath a smokescreen of Spanish moss to the busy street. The patterns created by the shadows of the great oaks make it easy to understand why Simeon Smith named his home Shadowlawn.

Almost directly across West Main Street from Shadowlawn stands Asbury Methodist Church, at 907 West Main.

Asbury Methodist Church

Franklin's oldest church, Asbury Methodist, was constructed by the congregation of the Ironside Baptist Church in 1838 on land that had been donated by Michael Gordy. Ownership of the land and the structure reverted to Gordy's heirs when the church closed its doors during the War Between the States. In 1866 it was purchased by the Parent Missionary Society of the Methodist-Episcopal Church in New York for the black congregation of the Asbury Methodist Church.

The building was restored in 1900 and in 1968 after hurricanes. Though they began their ministry in the older Bayou Sale Baptist Church, the Reverends Baynard C. Robert and Peter W. Robert preached at the Ironside Baptist Church for many years. They were two of the first Baptist ministers ever ordained in Louisiana.

Continue on West Main from Asbury Methodist Church for half a block, and turn left on Iberia Street. Drive two blocks and turn left onto Second Street. Drive half a block to the Smith House (on the right) at 909 Second.

Smith House

The walkway to the Smith House (private) is dotted with islands of greenery and leads beneath a forest of oaks and magnolias. The three-story structure is of brick below and cypress above. The lower porch is level with the ground, and from it rise six round columns covered with ivy. Six smaller columns line the upper gallery, which is enclosed by a white, green-trimmed balustrade. The doors of each level are ornamented by fanlights.

The Smith house once contained Franklin's first bank.

The Isaac Trowbridge house has remained in the same family since its construction in 1834.

The Smith House was built by John Hartman in about 1832. From 1837 to 1847 the basement of the house served as a branch of the New Orleans Canal and Banking Company and was operated by W. T. Palfrey, the owner during that period.[8] The home was purchased in 1848 by Dr. James Smith, and it remained in the Smith family for the next seventy years. Davy Crockett is said to have spent a night here on his way to Texas, where the statesman and adventurer died at the Alamo. Union General Godfrey Weitzel made the home his Franklin headquarters, and at times troops were quartered upstairs while their horses occupied the lower floor. The Smith House was completely restored in 1924 by New Orleans architect Morgan D. White for the (then) owner Paul Kramer.

Continue along Second Street to Adams. Turn left, and after one block turn right on First Street to drive half a block to the Isaac Trowbridge House (on the left) at 808 First Street.

Isaac Trowbridge House

Four square columns front both galleries of the Isaac Trowbridge House (private), and each gallery is enclosed by a white, wooden balustrade. The upper gallery is now screened, and a large dormer with two sets of windows breaks the slope of the roof. The home was built in 1834 by Isaac Trowbridge, and it has remained (1978) in the possession of the Trowbridge family.

Just across the street from the Trowbridge House stands St. Mary's Episcopal Church, at 805 First Street.

St. Mary's Episcopal Church

St. Mary's Episcopal Church was completed in 1872, after the 1870 fire that destroyed the original 1849 building. The church's large bell dates to the 1860s. The main roofline, the roofline over the entrance, and the four tiny gables of the steeple are all ornamented with gingerbread trim. The large side windows are equipped with louvered shutters. Particularly impressive is the beautiful woodwork (in white and two shades of green) of the rounded choir loft and of the stairway which leads to it.

> From the church drive two and a half blocks along First Street, crossing Jackson and Commercial, to the corner of Parkerson. At this intersection is the Bonino House at 300 Parkerson.

Bonino House

Bonino House (private) was built in the 1830s by André Cressen, and it served as a store with living quarters above. It has been in the possession of the Bonino family since 1870. The weatherboarded house is in a rather bad state of repair at the moment. Brick steps lead from the ground to the door, sheltered by the gallery above. Five square columns support this gallery, and five more support the eaves of the roof above it.

> Continue on First Street to Willow Street. Turn right and drive one block to Second Street. Turn right and drive one-half block to 607 Second Street (on the left).

Chadwick Cottage, dating to the 1850s, has recently been restored.

The old home at 607 Second Street in Franklin now serves as an apartment house.

607 Second Street

Six short fluted Corinthian columns line the single gallery of this old home (private). A balustrade of white with green trim encloses the gallery and ends with two square engaged columns at the front two corners of the main structure. Now an apartment building, the home was constructed in 1854 by Jules G. Olivier, a banker. It was restored in 1940 by E. A. Boudreaux.

> From 607 Second Street, drive to the end of the block and turn left on Jackson Street. Drive one block, turn left on Third Street, and drive to the house (on the right) at 615 Third Street.

Chadwick Cottage

It is believed that Chadwick Cottage (private) was built in the early 1850s by Isaac Trowbridge, who in 1834 had built the home at 808 First Street in Franklin. Trowbridge sold the home in 1879 to Charles Chadwick, who occupied it until his death in 1949. He had adopted his infant niece, Sara Chadwick (nee Battarbee) in 1892, and she also lived in Chadwick Cottage until 1971. George B. Thomson purchased the cottage that year and provided a thorough restoration.

Brick steps lead to the cottage's single gallery, which is lined by six square columns and a spindled balustrade. The window facings are of Classic design, and the doorway features transom and sidelights. The gable roof is covered with cedar shakes.

From Chadwick Cottage, drive to the end of the block and turn right on Willow Street. Drive two blocks, turn right on Anderson, and drive to Adams Street. Turn left and park in front of Hanson School. On the school grounds directly behind the main building stands Eaglesfield.

Eaglesfield

Eaglesfield (private), which now houses the choral and home economics departments of Hanson School, was the plantation home of Hiram Anderson until 1859, when he sold it to Dr. James Fontaine. A later owner was Thomas Eaglesfield, from whom the home takes its name. The last to occupy the house was Mrs. Minnie Hanson Conolly, who donated it to the Hanson School. The portico is pedimented, and four square columns front each of the two galleries.

Leave Eaglesfield by Hale Street and turn right on Anderson Street. Drive to Adams Street, turn left, and drive to Rugby (on the right) at 609 Adams.

Rugby

The pedimented portico of Rugby (private) is flanked by dormer windows. Four square columns front the two galleries, the doorway is adorned with a blocking course, and the pediment features a Palladian fan window. The entrance features transom and sidelights, and the upper gallery is now screened.

Rugby was built of cypress in 1859 by the Reverend J. W. Dunn. Under his direction it served as an Episcopal boarding school for boys until the outbreak of the War Between the States. It was acquired in 1869 by Alfred Gates, whose family owned it for many years. When St. Mary's Episcopal Church burned in 1870, services were held in Rugby until the new church was completed in 1872. J. J. Pringle, a noted sportsman of his day, leased the home for use as a hunting lodge from 1885 to 1893.

Continue on Adams Street to Main Street. Turn left and drive 0.5 mile to Sterling Road (Highway 322). Turn right and drive 0.3 mile to the Grevemberg House.

Right above: *Rugby, once a boarding school, is now a private home.*

Right: *The old Grevemberg house now contains the St. Mary Parish Museum.*

The Grevemberg House

This old home stands in the center of Franklin City Park, and it now contains the St. Mary Parish Museum. The structure was probably built in 1851 or soon thereafter by one Henry C. Wilson, who sold it in 1857 to Mrs. Gabriel Grevemberg. A later resident was Donelson Caffery, Jr., son of Senator Donelson Caffery, whose old home called Haifleigh once stood nearby.

Four fluted Corinthian columns support the pediment and front the two galleries of the Greek Revival Grevemberg House. The pediment and cornices are ornamented with a dentil course, and the upper gallery is enclosed by a spindled balustrade. The doorway of each gallery, rather than being centered, is offset to the viewer's right side of the facade. The rear of the home features a one-story loggia with two square columns.

The home was restored in 1973 by the St. Mary Chapter of the Louisiana Landmarks Society, and the museum opened that year. Inside are fine paintings and antiques, most on loan from members of the society. Visitors will see the original high and handsome wooden window facings and door facings, marble mantels, and the original cypress flooring. Of special interest are the flag of the St. Mary Cannoneers, captured by Union forces in the Battle of Irish Bend, and the coats-of-arms of many of the old families of Bayou Teche. The museum is open 3:00 p.m. to 5:00 p.m. on Tuesday and Thursday, and 1:00 p.m. to 5:00 p.m. on Saturday and Sunday.

Drive 5.2 miles farther along the west bank of Bayou Teche on Sterling Road (La. 322 and Parish 28) to Oaklawn Manor. Sterling Road follows a loop in Bayou Teche which was named Irish Bend years ago in honor of Alexander Porter, an Irishman, who built Oaklawn Manor.

BATTLE OF IRISH BEND

The Battle of Bisland near Patterson had occurred on the evening of April 12 and the day of April 13, 1863. One-third of Union General Nathaniel Banks's force had traveled by boat through Grand Lake to land on the Teche above Franklin, while the main force had moved up the Teche from Berwick to catch the forces of General Dick Taylor in a deadly trap. Confederate resistance foiled the plan by delaying the landing of the Federal troops from Grand Lake.

When General Taylor received word on the evening of April 13 that the Yankees had established a foothold on the Teche near Oaklawn Manor, he abandoned Bisland under cover of darkness and withdrew to Franklin, arriving about 2 a.m. on April 14. He sent his wagons to Baldwin, and his troops marched to the great loop of Bayou Teche above Franklin, called Irish Bend, where they deployed just before dawn in the unharvested sugarcane fields to wait.

The Union forces had crossed the bridge at Oaklawn Manor on the evening of April 13 and camped on the plantation grounds (taking Madame Porter's son captive). The ten thousand Union soldiers began their two-mile march at daylight on April 14. They were stopped short at Irish Bend by heavy gunfire and by shelling from the gunboat Diana (which had been damaged at Bisland but quickly repaired).

After a rush on the St. Mary (Parish) Cannoneers, the Union forces withdrew to care for their four hundred killed and wounded. Taylor returned to Franklin to begin the withdrawal of men and materiel (leaving General Alfred Mouton of Lafayette in charge at the battle line). The Confederates crossed the Bayou Yokely Bridge, burned it, and marched to Jeanerette.[9] In General Taylor's own words, "We didn't lose a dishpan"[10] (though there had been some Confederate casualties, of course). Trapped between two Union armies on Bayou Teche, the Confederate gunboats (including the Diana) were sunk to prevent capture.

OAKLAWN MANOR

Oaklawn Manor was built by Alexander Porter of Donegal County, Ireland. Porter was a representative at Louisiana's Constitutional Convention in 1811 and 1812, a member of the state legislature in 1816 and 1817, and a U.S. senator from 1833 to 1844. He began purchasing the lands of Oaklawn in 1812, and construction of the home was begun in 1837. It was at a meeting at Oaklawn that Porter founded the Whig party of Louisiana.

Porter died in 1844, his widow left the home in 1881, and there followed a long period of neglect. Captain Clyde A. Barbour, who as captain of a bayou steamer passed the lovely home and grounds around the turn of the century, swore to buy Oaklawn one day. In 1925 he became the owner. The home burned in 1926 during restoration, and it was Barbour who rebuilt it (from the walls, columns, lower galleries, and huge cypress beams that remained). The cypress flooring of the lower floor was replaced with square marble tiles from the old St. Charles

Oaklawn Manor stands beside Bayou Teche in the world's largest grove of live oaks.

Hotel in New Orleans, which had burned in 1868.[11] The most recent restoration was conducted by the George B. Thomson family in 1964.

Oaklawn is open to visitors from 8:30 a.m. to 5:00 p.m. daily. From the entrance to the property, a winding drive leads to the mansion through the gardens and oak grove beside Bayou Teche. The gardens were designed by a French landscape architect, and the seventy-five-acre grove of oaks is said to be the largest in the world, despite the fact that some of the ancient trees have fallen before hurricanes. Most of the oaks are believed to be more than three hundred years old, but one hundred of them (now over fifty years old) were added by Captain Barbour. The drive passes fountains and Greek statuary. The long alley of red cedars here is said to be unique in America. The trees, brought by Porter from Tennessee, lead from near the main gate to the manor.

Six columns with smooth Tuscan capitals front the Greek Colonial mansion. Seven steps lead between two giant urns to the gallery, beneath a balcony which spans the width of the facade. Double windows open onto another much smaller balcony, which is set into the huge pediment. Both balconies are enclosed by black ironwork. On one side of the home is a covered carriage drive by a side entrance. Steps in the rear of the home lead up to a flagstone patio that features a sunken pool with a marble fountain. The rear of Oaklawn is identical to the front, but a large wing is attached with six columns lining its two galleries. The wing once contained the old kitchen downstairs and a *garçonnière* above.

Still in existence are original brick walkways that leave the manor to ramble along the cedar walk and through the three main gardens. To one side of the big house stands the little butterhouse, rebuilt with its original bricks and fronted by double, shuttered doors with a tiny

fanlight. Inside is a well two feet in diameter which is bricked as far down as one can see. Here also is kept Alexander Porter's old bathtub, carved from one gigantic block of marble. Near the butterhouse stands a handsome aviary, built in 1974 for the filming of a detective movie called *The Drowning Pool*, which starred Paul Newman.

Behind the manor is the old carriage house, equipped with living quarters upstairs, which is now used as a spacious garage. Nearby stands the old milk house, unchanged since the days of Alexander Porter. Here passes the trench which Porter had dug for the drainage of his land. Today it drains the large swimming pool, which is shaded by two oak trees, each about three hundred years old.

Visitors enter the home by the carriage entrance and are met by guides. Nearby, at the intersection of two hallways, two fluted Doric miniatures reach from the marble floor to the ceiling. The main hallway is usually brilliant with sunlight from the oversized fanlights of the doors at each end. Fine antiques, chandeliers of every description, and oil paintings, including one of Alexander Porter, fill the rooms of this lovely home. A singular chandelier of Venetian glass graces one of the rooms of the main floor. One moment a highly ornate, marble-topped gold table catches the visitor's eye, and the next moment his attention is drawn through a huge archway to the dining room and drawing room with their matching French crystal chandeliers. The mantels throughout the mansion include marble from Belgium and Italy. Persian rugs extend the lengths of the marble halls, and on one wall hangs a large painting of a young girl, *Salome*, which creates the illusion that her eyes, face, and entire body face the observer no matter where he stands.

Tours do not include the second and third floors of Oaklawn. On the second floor is the room named for Henry Clay, who visited in 1842. Here are a desk of African mahogany

Attached to Oaklawn's rear galleries is the old rear wing that served as kitchen and garconniere.

with inlayed designs, an etching of Clay addressing the Senate, a cradle from Oak Alley Plantation on the Mississippi, a marble mantel, a giant armoire of rosewood, and a large rosewood tester bed with unusual corner ornamentation. The third floor once housed a ballroom that measured ninety-two feet.

Return by the drive to Parish 28 and turn right. Drive 3.5 miles to Highway 182, turn right, and drive 2.4 miles to a small sign (on the right) that calls attention to the Baldwin branch of the St. Mary Bank and Trust. The driveway beneath this sign leads to the old house called Darby, the basement of which now houses the bank.

Darby, circa 1765. Its basement is now a drive-in bank.

DARBY

Darby, in the heart of the town of Baldwin, is fronted by six columns of rounded brick, covered with hand-smoothed plaster, which support the gallery, and by six cypress colonettes which support the steep hipped roof of ancient wood shingles. Two dormer windows and two chimneys interrupt the slope of the roof. Two stairways lead to the gallery, one from the front (unsheltered), and one from beneath the gallery.

The house is of the French West Indies type and was built around 1765 by an early settler of the region. Nearby, until the 1960s, stood a home called Fuselier, completed in 1803, which was modeled after Darby but which is considerably larger. It has since been moved by barge to the east bank of Bayou Teche near Jeanerette. François Darby became the owner of the older home in 1856, and a later resident was John Baldwin, for whom the town is named. The St. Mary Bank has occupied the lower floor since 1969.

Return by Darby's driveway to Highway 182 and turn right. Drive one block to the traffic light, and turn left on Highway 83. From the light it is 4.0 miles to the intersection of Parish Highway 30. A driveway leads left from this intersection, through the white gates of Vacherie Plantation to the old home called Vacherie. The home and the driveway that leads to it are private, and this information is provided only for the purpose of documenting the existence and location of the home.

VACHERIE

The original section of Vacherie (private) was built as early as 1816 by Gregoire Bodin at the time of his first marriage. In 1841 after his first wife died, he remarried and built another home, only a short distance from the first, on land that was not part of the community property from his first marriage. His first home was then placed atop the new one, forming the two-and-one-half-story structure that stands today.[12]

Six Doric columns of brick line the lower gallery, while eleven wooden colonettes front the upper gallery. The lower, of brick, is flush with the ground, which was common in houses whose locations were not in danger of flooding. Louvered shutters adorn the doors and windows of the two main floors, while the attic windows feature board shutters.

Return to Baldwin by Highway 83, cross Highway 182 at the traffic light onto Highway 326 (the Charenton Road), and drive 2.6 miles from the light to the unusual and interesting home called the Albert Heaton House.

ALBERT HEATON HOUSE

Of board and batten construction, the Albert

Heaton House (private) consists of a two-story central section which is flanked by two one-story wings. A single gallery fronts the house, while the facade of the bayou side includes a portico that is enclosed by an attractive balustrade. The home is gray, and the shutters of the French doors are turquoise.

The home was constructed by Albert Heaton on the Irish Bend Road near Franklin in 1853. The Italian design was created by Alexander Davis, an important architect of the nineteenth century. Davis headed a firm in New York where James Gallier was employed for a time. Gallier and his son later made New Orleans their home, and they designed many of the finest public buildings and plantation homes of the city and state.

Heaton House was sold in 1854 to George Runk, and it remained in the Runk family for nearly one hundred years. It was purchased in 1966 by Mr. and Mrs. H. H. Dinkins who had it moved fifteen miles by barge to its present location. The design had been recognized by Samuel Wilson, Jr., a respected restoration architect of the firm of Koch and Wilson in New Orleans, and it was he who directed the restoration of the home.

The ceilings of many of the rooms of the Heaton House still boast their original white, sectioned cypress panels. In one front room beneath old wallpaper was found an 1857 issue

The old Albert Heaton house, an Italian villa on Bayou Teche.

of the New Orleans *Weekly Delta*, which had apparently been used as a backing for the wallpaper. The newspaper has been glassed over and framed. In the master bedroom is an excellent half tester bed of unusually ornate design. From the front room of the central section of the home rises a graceful curving stairway, with banister and hand-carved octagonal spindles of walnut. Part of one upstairs wall has been left uncovered to show the circular saw marks that were made by some unknown laborer in the mid-nineteenth century.

Drive back to the town of Baldwin, and turn right on Highway 182 at the traffic light. It is 7.8 miles from the light to Albania Mansion, which stands just down the bayou from the town of Jeanerette.

ALBANIA MANSION

Albania is open to the public, and it contains one of the finest collections of antiques in Louisiana. The driveway takes visitors to the old carriage entrance, where the facade includes six large, square columns that rise from the lower gallery to support the upper gallery and the dormered roof. Balustrades of white, trimmed in green, enclose both galleries, and louvered shutters adorn the windows and doors with their handsome facings. The gallery windows are of an unusual type, like those of Idlewild near Patterson. The shutters open to expose little two-foot doors beneath the high windows.

Vacherie, built in two sections for two wives.

One may open the windows only for a breeze, or the windows and the tiny doors to create additional passageways. The sides of the three-story home are enhanced by traditional shuttered windows.

This is a house with two fronts. Opposite the carriage entrance is the bayou entrance, equally important or perhaps more important in the era of the construction of the mansion. On this side is a portico, consisting of two levels, with balustrades and four more of the large columns. Set back over the portico is a pediment flanked by dormer windows. A few feet from the home, on the lawn which leads down to the bayou, is the salvaged anchor of the Confederate gunboat *Queen of the West*.

Construction of Albania was begun in 1837 and ended in 1842. The builder was Charles François Grevemberg, and the cypress came from his own lands. Grevemberg arrived in Louisiana around 1792, and he received land grants from Louis XVI and Napoleon I, which are recorded in the archives of the courthouse in New Orleans. Grevemberg married Euphemie Fuselier, of a family of French Royalist refugees who had settled on Bayou Teche. Both were killed at the grand resort hotel at Last Island during the storm of August, 1856, which leveled everything on the island and killed the vast majority of those vacationing there.

Grevemberg's only surviving son was reared at Albania by a grandmother, but when the boy was 19, the estate was sold to Samuel and Isaac Delgado. The boy's grandson, Francis C. Grevemberg, became the head of the Louisiana

Albania Mansion, completed in 1842. Huge square columns dominate the twin galleries of the "carriage front" of the home.

Below: *Adrien Persac's painting of Albania, executed in 1861, depicts the bayou side of the mansion. Also shown are servant quarters and garconnieres, and the old cistern that still remains. (Courtesy of Mrs. Edward J. Gilly of New Orleans.)*

Bottom: *The "bayou front" of Albania features a columned portico.*

State Police under Governor Kennon. The Delgados acquired the property and home in 1885. Samuel died first, and before Isaac's death in 1909 he willed the lands and home of Albania to the city of New Orleans, which was instructed to use the revenue for the operation of the trade school that bears Delgado's name in that city. That is the situation as it still exists, though the home was bought at public auction by Mr. and Mrs. James H. Bridges in 1957.

The focal point of Albania's great hallway is the impressive stairway that winds its way, unsupported, to the third floor. A small and pretty chandelier hangs from a plaster medallion just past the stairway. Nearby hang the Grevemberg crest and iron reproductions of the old Grevemberg cattle brands.

The first two rooms to the right of the hall are the double parlors, where crystal chandeliers hang from intricate plaster medallions. In the first parlor is a Venetian mirror in an exquisitely carved frame, which dates to 1841, and a Brambach piano dating to 1895. The handsome mantel in the second parlor is one of eight in the home, all marble.

Across the hallway from the parlors is the Napoleon Room. Here are an attractive colonial four-poster bed and a seven-piece set, featuring carved swans, which dates to 1793. The set includes a marriage couch and was owned, it is said, by Bonaparte himself. Farther down the hall is the master bedroom with its handsome furnishings and library, with a large collection of books on Napoleon. One of these is a first edition by Alexandre Dumas that dates to 1840, with hand-tinted prints throughout.

Visitors may climb the remarkable winding stairway to the second floor. In the Rosewood Room are five pieces of furniture that have been here since the construction of Albania. Many of the rooms have small dressing rooms attached, and the one in the Rosewood Room features a display of pre–Civil War clothing and other items of interest. In the French and Lilac Rooms are more fine antiques. The Bayou Room overlooks Bayou Teche, and sunlight from the large windows adds brightness to the gay colors of the Oriental rug and the upholstery of the furniture. Next to the Bayou Room is the Doll Room, so named because it houses Mrs. Bridges' famous one-thousand-doll collection, the product of twenty-five years of effort. One is a joss doll, made prior to 1643. The dolls are beautiful and should be of interest to those of any age, gender, and disposition.

A ghost, we are told, either occupies or occasionally visits Albania. She is middle-aged and a bit chubby, and she has reportedly been seen in her antebellum garb by residents and a number of guests through the years.

On the grounds of Albania Mansion can be found an old building that was formerly a slave cabin. It is now air-conditioned and furnished with antiques, and it contains a modern kitchen. Arrangements for overnight or lengthier stays in the pleasant cabin can be made (no later than a day in advance) by calling (318) 276–4816.

From Albania it is 0.6 mile up the bayou to Lewis Street in the town of Jeanerette. Turn right on Lewis (Highway 3182), and drive to the Old Faye Home (on the left) numbered 217.

JEANERETTE AREA

This town was named for John W. Jeanerette, who on February 25, 1830, opened the first post office between New Iberia and Charenton. The office was in his home, Beau Pré, which is just up the bayou from the town. He also served for a time as justice of the peace. The town was incorporated in 1878, with J. E. Provost serving as the first mayor.

Jeanerette is located in the heart of one of the most productive sugarcane areas of the world. Five sugar mills, in fact, stand within walking distance of the little town.[13]

Old Faye Home

This home is now owned (1978) by Miss Mae Faye. Her great-grandfather, Denis Faye, owned a plantation that lay two miles east of Jeanerette, where he built this house for his son Alexandre. The son brought his bride to the home, and by the time the War Between the States broke out he was the father of four children. This means that the home was built no later than about 1857, and probably earlier. The plantation and home were lost after the War, and the new owners had the house moved into town. It was Miss Faye's father who regained the home by purchase, bringing it back into the original family.

Six ornate colonettes line the single gallery of the Old Faye Home, and three shuttered dormers line the gable roof. The doorway features transom and sidelights.

Return to Main Street and turn right. Drive several blocks through downtown Jeanerette and turn left onto Highway 85. After 1.4 miles, Highway 85 turns right. Follow it 1.9 miles to the point where it turns left again, and from here it is 1.5 miles (crossing U.S. 90) on Highway 85 to the intersection of Highway

Enterprise, built circa 1835 by Simeon Patout, remains a possession of the Patout family.

673 in Patoutville. Turn left on 673 and drive 0.7 mile to Patout Road. Turn left and drive 0.6 mile to Enterprise. Enterprise and the road that leads to it are private, and this information is provided only for the purpose of documenting the existence and location of the home.

Enterprise

Enterprise (private) is set in a formal garden, and attractive lampposts stand here and there among the plants. Two galleries front the home, with six columns of brick below and six of wood above. The lower gallery is ground level, and it is floored with bricks laid in the herringbone design. A wing has been added to the original structure.

Enterprise was constructed about 1835 by Simeon Patout from Usay, France. He had been given a royal French land grant to develop a wine industry, but he found the climate and soil here unsuitable for grapes. He resorted, subsequently, to the staple crop of sugarcane. The present owners (1978) are Mr. and Mrs. William Schwing Patout, Jr.

Enterprise was once set on high brick foundations, but these have been enclosed to form today's lower floor. Near the main door of the lower gallery is another door that opens onto a stairway leading inside to the second floor. There are four main rooms and a hallway on each floor, all with beautifully paneled ceilings. The main stairway is of mahogany.

The old double parlors upstairs now serve as bedrooms. In one is an antique tester bed from France, and in the other is a Mallard bed, purchased in New Orleans in the 1830s. The rear of the home features a portico that is supported by two brick columns and covered with Confederate jasmine. One of the two original *garçonnières* remains, and it stands nearby.

Return via the Patout Road to Highway 673, turn right, and drive to Highway 85. Drive 1.5 miles (crossing U.S. 90 again) to the point where Highway 85 turns right. Follow it for 1.9 miles, turn left, and drive 1.4 miles to Main Street in Jeanerette. Turn left and drive one block to Highway 3-182. Turn right, cross the Bayou Teche bridge, and follow the road on the far side that curves to your right. Park beside the road, immediately around this curve, and walk to see the old cemetery atop an ancient Indian mound beside the bayou.

Here you will see the grave of John Gaulden Richardson, who fought in the Battle of New Orleans. Here also are his sons, Francis and John, and their wives. Francis was the builder of Bayside Plantation House, which is your next stop. John built Westover.

Turn around at the Indian mound and return to the bridge. Without crossing the bridge, turn right to follow Bayou Teche on Highway 87. It is a small fraction of a mile to Bayside, which stands facing the bayou from a hill on the right.

Bayside brings beauty to the east bank of Bayou Teche near Jeanerette.

Bayside

Named for the trees that surround the home, Bayside (private) was built in the Greek Revival style. The two-story white brick structure is fronted by upper and lower galleries. On the upper gallery, an ornate wooden balustrade runs along the bays between the six Doric columns, which are set on high pedestals. The transoms and sidelights of the doors are set into recesses in the thick walls.

The Richardson family acquired this land in 1845, and Francis Richardson built his home in 1850. He was a state legislator prior to the war, and he had been a friend and classmate of Edgar Allan Poe. He is credited with having floated a barge of burning hay in the path of Union gunboats on Bayou Teche during the Bayou Country Campaign.

Bayside is now furnished with English antiques. The floor of the lower hallway has been replaced, but those of the other rooms are still of the original cypress boards. The cypress doors throughout the home, with their brass fixtures, are also original, as is the oak stairway. In the double parlors are fine marble mantels which were added in the early 1900s, and Waterford crystal chandeliers hang from old plaster medallions. The small wing that houses the office and library is an addition to the original structure.

The upper, rear gallery has been enclosed for children's rooms. The walls of these rooms are of wide boards from a huge pine that had stood in the backyard before it was downed by Hurricane Hilda. Large square columns line the remaining rear gallery. Near the old plantation bell behind the home stands a mill house that is as old as Bayside.

Leaving Bayside, you must drive 0.5 mile farther along Highway 87 to Fuselier.

Fuselier

Construction of Fuselier (private) was begun in 1796 and completed in 1803. It was built by a French Royalist refugee named Agricolé de la Claire. The structure first stood in Baldwin near the older home called Darby, from which it was modeled. It was moved by barge in 1961 to its present location, where it became the home of J. Randolph Roane, great-great-great-nephew of Fuselier's builder.

The two-and-one-half-story home, of the French West Indies style, is topped by two chimneys and two dormer windows. Cedar shakes have replaced the original cypress shingles of the hipped roof. The lower floor is built of brick, and the upper is weatherboarded *bousillage*. Six round, plastered columns of handmade bricks support the gallery, which is lined with eight colonettes and a balustrade.

Each floor of Fuselier was originally three rooms wide and one deep, but the three rooms on the lower floor have been converted into two larger ones. The bricks of the walls of the lower section were taken apart and recemented at the time of the move, and they have been braced with steel supports. The floors of this section are of the original hexagonal Spanish tiles. The rear galleries are now enclosed by large windows. The bath house, standing next to the pool behind the home, is a small replica of Fuselier.

Turn around at Fuselier and drive back, passing Bayside again, to the bridge. Cross the bayou and turn right on Highway 182. It is 0.3 mile to Westover (on the right). One great Louisiana writer, Frances Parkinson Keyes, called this drive "one of the loveliest stretches of country road in Louisiana."[14]

Westover

The front and side galleries of Westover are lined with square columns, and the side galleries are now screened. The windows feature green louvered shutters, and the windows and doors are adorned with attractive facings. The two-story home was constructed in 1860 by John Wesley Richardson, brother of the builder of Bayside.

From Westover it is 0.8 mile along Highway 182 to Loisel.

Loisel

Loisel Plantation was built in 1830 by Nicholas

Fuselier, completed in 1803 in the town of Baldwin, was moved by barge on Bayou Teche to its present location near Jeanerette.

Loisel, and it was purchased in 1877 by Harvey Burleigh. Nine square columns line the long gallery of Loisel, now shaded by modern awning beneath the eaves of the dormered roof. Green latticework fills the spaces between the brick foundations, and three interesting additions to the home (each smaller than its predecessor) extend from the viewer's left side of the main structure. A beautiful setting is provided by the many oaks and pines of the large yard.

From Loisel it is 1.1 miles via Highway 182 to Beau Pré.

Beau Pré

Fronted by a screened gallery with four columns, Beau Pré (private) is topped by heavy green Spanish tile on the main roof, as well as on the roof of the gallery. The large yard is enclosed by a white iron fence, and the gates bear the name of the home.

This two-story house with its one-story gallery exemplifies a style that was popular in the Carolinas during the 1790s and early 1800s. The type is more common to North Louisiana and the Florida Parishes than to the Bayou Country, as can be explained by migration and settlement patterns of the early nineteenth century.

Originally named Pine Grove, the home was constructed in 1829 by Thomas H. Thompson as a wedding gift for his daughter. In 1830 it was purchased by John W. Jeanerette, for whom the nearby town was named. The home is surrounded by large pines, magnolias, and oaks, and Jeanerette was inspired to name it Beau Pré ("beautiful prairie").

From Beau Pré, drive 2.9 miles farther along Highway 182 to the driveway of the Jacob S. Landry home. This home and the drive that leads to it are private, and this information is provided only for the purpose of documenting the existence and location of the home.

LANDRY HOME

The central portion of this home is thought to be about 150 years old, though no definite dates are known, and it is believed to have been built by an Olivier family. The house stands on land that was once part of a plantation called Orange Grove, but whether or not this was the manor is unknown.

The older section of the structure consists of the central rooms, fronted by a single gallery (now screened) with four one-story Doric columns. The original cypress flooring is intact. The home is furnished with many fine antiques, but the piece most treasured—and understandably so—is an armoire which was a gift of Weeks Hall. Mr. Hall was the last private owner of the beautiful and famous home in New Iberia called Shadows-on-the-Teche, and he was a frequent visitor in the Landry home.

From the entrance to the Landry home, it is 4.1 miles up Highway 182 to the old home (on the left) at 544 East Main Street in New Iberia.

NEW IBERIA AREA

It was in 1779 that some sixteen families of Spaniards from Malaga, led by Francisco Bouligni of the Spanish military in Louisiana, were sent to this area by Governor Bernardo de Galvez to establish a colony. Word came in August of that year that Spain had declared war with Great Britain, so Spanish Louisiana was suddenly an American ally in the Revolutionary War. Fifteen of the Malagueños marched away with Bouligni to assist Governor Galvez, and they participated in the now famous "Marcha de Galvez," which resulted in the fall of British forts in Manchac and Baton Rouge.[15]

Named in honor of the Iberian Peninsula, Bouligni's settlement prospered. It was incorporated in 1836, and when Iberia Parish was established in 1868, it became the parish seat. The town, with its surrounding area, is a year-round tourist attraction, but its popularity reaches a peak during the annual Louisiana Sugarcane Festival, held in September.[16]

544 Main Street

This home (private) was built late in the eighteenth century, and it is thought by many to be the oldest house in New Iberia. It was moved to its present location from the heart of town in 1883 by a man named Ledbetter. The weatherboarded house is fronted by a short gallery, now screened, which is lined with four square, wooden columns.

The home is filled with charming relics of the past. There are beautiful Persian rugs, marble mantels, the original wide cypress board flooring, and many fine pieces of antique furniture. The structure is supported by two-foot-by-two-foot cypress beams, forty feet long.

Just across the street from 544 East Main is the house numbered 541 East Main.

Gebert Oak

The home at 541 East Main (private) is practically hidden from the street by the huge live oak that stands in the center of the large front yard. The tree was planted between 1831 and 1835 by a Mrs. Jason Marsh over the graves of her twin children. While the oak is not so very old by Louisiana standards, its limbspan is one of the most magnificent in the state, covering the large lawn almost entirely. It is called the Gebert Oak and is, of course, a member of the Louisiana Live Oak Society.

A few blocks farther along East Main from the Gebert Oak, on the left, stands the First Federal Savings and Loan Company.

First Federal Building

The gallery of First Federal Savings and Loan, with its four fluted Doric columns, is new, but the original structure behind the facade was built just after the War Between the States, perhaps in 1870. Called the Old Fontelieu House, it was the home of one of New Iberia's early mayors. The beautiful old bricks on the

sides of the building bespeak the structure's true age.

Shadows-on-the-Teche

Across Main Street from the First Federal Building, in a spacious lawn surrounded by a high white fence, stands the most famous home on Bayou Teche and one of Louisiana's most beautiful—the Shadows-on-the-Teche. The home singlehandedly attracts many of the tourists who come into the Bayou Country yearly. If the Shadows is the only home they visit in Louisiana, they could not choose one that is better preserved, more authentically restored, more charmingly and accurately furnished, or

A rear view of the Shadows, as it appears from Bayou Teche.

more symbolic of that splendid era before the tragic war.

This three-story, sixteen-room mansion is a flawless example of the Classic Revival architectural style as it was adapted to the climate and conditions of Louisiana by the wealthy landowners of the early and middle nineteenth century. Eight Doric columns, beautifully tapered and set on high, separate pedestals, rise to support an entablature of breathtaking Classic woodwork.

The first floor and its gallery are flush with the ground and are floored with bricks laid in the herringbone design. The stairway that rises from the first to the second gallery is sheltered by one of the jalousies that shade each end of both galleries. The elegant simplicity of the stairway's green-trimmed white railing is repeated in the balustrade of the second-floor gallery. Two doors and three green-shuttered windows open onto each of the galleries.

While age bestows beauty on any brick home, the pink bricks of the Shadows have been given a unique treatment by nature, and they seem to glow. Two chimneys break the peak, and six dormer windows (three on the front and three on the bayou side) break the slope of the slate roof. Also on the bayou side are first-floor and second-floor loggias. The lower is fronted by three arches in brick, and the upper is enclosed by a short balustrade and two small Doric columns. A small stairway, formerly for servants, rises from the lower level to the upper. There are no indoor stairways, since these were taxable luxuries when the Shadows was constructed.

The lovely lawn that surrounds the Shadows is shaded by live oaks and cedars that were planted, along with the camellias, in the 1830s by the wife of the builder. Walkways of handmade bricks lead to the old kitchen and slave quarters and wind through the formal garden. On one side of the house stands a sundial, cast in 1827, on which an inscription states that "abundance is the daughter of economy and hard work." Near the corners of the home stand statues of the four seasons.

The high, white fence that borders the lawn along Main Street is a reproduction of the original copied from Adrien Persac's painting of the home, executed in 1861. He painted the bayou side as well as the street side of the Shadows, and today these paintings hang in the home's formal dining room.

William Weeks, an Englishman, arrived in the area that is now the Feliciana Parishes of Louisiana in 1792, or shortly therebefore, and soon received a large land grant on Bayou Teche. He sent his son, David, to develop the property. The holdings of David Weeks, who had married Mary Clara Conrad, soon grew to

The Shadows-on-the-Teche, as it appears from Main Street in New Iberia.

include the plantations of Grand Cote, Cypremort, Parc Perdu, Vermilion Bridge, Richohoc and Acadia. Grand Cote was later renamed Weeks Island. It is said that David Weeks had picked his homesite in 1825, but the baking of the bricks did not begin until 1831. The architect was James Bedell, and the family occupied the Shadows in the spring of 1834. Weeks left immediately for the East Coast for reasons of health, and he died in Connecticut after only a few months. In 1841 his widow married Judge John Moore, who was elected that year to Congress.

Union General Nathaniel Banks made the Shadows his New Iberia headquarters during the Bayou Country Campaign, and Mrs. Moore, who refused to swear allegiance to the Union, was placed under house arrest and confined to the third floor of her home. When she died, the Shadows and other family property came under the control of William Weeks II, son of David Weeks. William's wife and two of his children had died in the tragic storm that destroyed the massive resort hotel of Last Island in August of 1856. The bodies of the children were recovered, and they are buried in the family cemetery in the southwest corner of the lawn. His only surviving child, a daughter, married Major Gilbert Hall, originally of New York, and this couple eventually occupied the old home.

The years after the war were, of course, a period of increasing debts and hard times. However, a great salt dome was discovered at Weeks Island, and the family home and lands were saved. The Shadows became known as "the house that sugar built and salt saved."

The Halls had one son, Weeks Hall, named for his famous ancestors. He served in World War I, but it was fifteen years before he saw his home again. He remained in Paris to study art after the war and returned to the Shadows in 1922 as a respected painter. He spent the rest of his life restoring and preserving the home and gardens. His many friends from around the world flocked to visit him at the Shadows, and a door, now in his old studio, bears the signatures of many of these. The door was once cleaned by a well-meaning maid, but the guests returned

again and again throughout the years so that most of the names were replaced. Some of the names that will catch your eye are H. L. Mencken, Stark Young, Cecil B. DeMille, Mae West, Walt Disney, Tex Ritter, Roark Bradford, and Lyle Saxon.

Saxon was a frequent visitor, and stories of happy times at the Shadows can be found in his book, *Some Friends of Joe Gilmore*. Saxon had this to say about the old home shortly after Hall's restoration of 1922:

> Now the house appears just as it did when it was built—only it is lovelier, for time has brought out new colors in the warm red-brick walls, and the garden has had a century to grow in. I can hardly describe the warm comforts of these bedrooms on a frosty day, when log fires are lighted on the hearth and when one is wakened by a man-servant bearing the coffee tray. One lies there, propped up in bed, sipping coffee, while the curtains are thrown back to admit the sunlight. I have never been able to decide whether the old house is more charming in winter by firelight and candlelight, or in summer, when the breeze from the bayou billows the curtains and causes the candles to flicker beneath their glass cylinders.[17]

That 1922 restoration was handled by Richard Koch of the New Orleans restoration firm of Armstrong and Koch. The mansion received major restoration again in 1961 by the firm of Koch and Wilson. Just before Weeks Hall's death in 1958, the Shadows was accepted by the National Trust for Historic Preservation. The National Trust is an organization that has been chartered by Congress to preserve certain of our nation's historic sites and buildings. The Trust is, in effect, only continuing Weeks Hall's own work at the Shadows, for, in his own words: "I have never considered myself anything but a trustee of something fine which chance put in my hands to preserve. Fine things are without value, in that they belong to those rare people who appreciate them beyond price. It is to those people that I should like to entrust this place."[18]

The Shadows-on-the-Teche is open daily from 9:00 a.m. to 4:30 p.m., and there is a nominal admission price. For those who are interested, hostesses will provide literature that lists other properties of the National Trust for

Historic Preservation, procedures for joining that organization, and advantages of membership.

The first floor of the Shadows contains displays of household tools from the earliest days of Louisiana's settlement. Though some of the home's furniture was gathered by the National Trust, many of the pieces are original. The furnishings consist of Chippendale and Hepplewhite from the late eighteenth century, of Sheraton from the early nineteenth century, and of the later American Empire style. Even fabrics and wallpaper have been replaced accurately through research into Weeks family papers.

The entire interior is resplendent with Classic woodwork and plaster work—cornices of acanthus-leaf design and fluted pilasters beside every doorway. One seems to feel the warmth and gaiety, and the sorrows as well, of the great family that the Shadows housed from 1834 to 1958. Weeks Hall's studio now contains a display of his paintings, as well as his collection of old Louisiana books—many autographed with personal notes.

Next door to the Shadows is a home called the Ned Weeks House, which was built in the early 1900s. This is a beautiful home of glowing white, and it is easy to see the influence of the Shadows on the design of the younger structure.

From the Shadows, continue driving west on Main Street. Cross Weeks Street and drive two more blocks to Bridge Street. Turn right and cross Bayou Teche. Turn left, immediately on the far side of the bridge, onto Front Street. On the right stands Mount Carmel Convent and Catholic School.

Mount Carmel

This interesting old building was occupied by the Sisters of Mount Carmel in 1872. Five of the nuns, led by Mother St. John of the Cross Ançoin, had arrived in New Iberia in 1870 and had started a school at that time. They made their move to the more spacious accommodations two years later. The building was probably constructed around 1830, but many modifications

Above: *The front of the Shadows, as seen by Adrien Persac in 1861. The handsome fence that encloses the lawn of the Shadows today was copied from this painting. (Courtesy of the National Trust for Historic Preservation.)*

Below: *Adrien Persac's painting of the bayou side of the Shadows, executed in 1861. (Courtesy of the National Trust for Historic Preservation.)*

have been made through the years. It was first the home of Henri Frederic Duperier, the man who was responsible for surveying New Iberia and handling its incorporation in 1836.

Twelve square columns of simulated stone line the two galleries of the building's facade. Certain sections of the galleries have been enclosed. The interior boasts high ceilings and stately woodwork.

Just past the convent, at 203 Front Street, at the corner of Johnson Street, stands the Jacques Lamperez House.

Lamperez House

The Lamperez House (private) is thought to have been built in 1839 by Santiago Lamperez, formerly a brick mason in Spain, who (tradition has it) married Josephine Don Jose Santa Maria of royal lineage. She was subsequently disowned by her family, and the young couple left for the new world, settling in New Iberia.[19]

The small structure, with walls of *bousillage* (covered with weatherboards), has the traditional louvered shutters and a tin roof. It is set

about two feet off the ground on brick foundations and cypress blocks. The old home is still (1978) in the Lamperez family.

From the Lamperez House, drive farther along Front Street to its dead end. Turn left onto the Jefferson Street bridge and cross the bayou. In the southwest corner of Main and Jefferson streets stands the Church of the Epiphany.

Church of the Epiphany

The cornerstone of the Church of the Epiphany was laid on October 15, 1857, on land donated by one Harvey Hopkins. It was completed the next year, and on May 16 it was consecrated by Bishop Leonidas K. Polk, Louisiana's first Episcopal bishop. The bishop was commissioned a general and gained fame in the War Between the States as "the fighting bishop of the Confederacy." Old church records show that the bishop baptised three adults and three children during his stay in New Iberia. The church was used as a field hospital and prison during Union occupation, and some say that it was also used to quarter horses. The pews were reportedly turned over to create improvised troughs.

This beautiful old brick building is partly covered with ivy, and the stained-glass Gothic windows along the sides are handsome ones. Inside, above the altar, are Tiffany stained-glass windows. Tiny spires rise from the front corners of the church, and the open, wooden steeple contains a huge old bell that can be seen from the street. The belfry and side buttresses were added in 1884, and the building was expanded to the rear in 1959.

Facing the side of Epiphany Church is the Magnolias, at 115 Jefferson Street.

The Magnolias

A two-level pedimented portico fronts the Magnolias, and on each level are two short, ornamented square columns. The upper level is enclosed by an attractive balustrade. Transomed doors and louvered shutters complete the facade.

New Iberia's Episcopal Church was consecrated by Bishop Leonidas Polk.

The Magnolias was built by a Dr. Stubinger and completed in 1852. Its cypress lumber came from huge trees selected in the nearby swamps and deadened in 1849. They were left standing for a year for natural curing before being cut and milled. The square-foot cypress beams, which run the length of the home underneath for support, are joined by wooden pegs. Minor additions have been made to the original eight rooms. The home first faced the bayou, but it was turned to face Jefferson Street in 1929. The twelve-foot-high walls of the front rooms reflect the ingenuity of the builders in that their lower three feet were built of brick—ratproof!

Dr. Stubinger had retained his British citizenship, and he flew the English flag during the War Between the States to prevent damage to his home and property. After his death, his home was used in turn as a hotel, a boarding house, and a peppersauce factory. It is now a private home again.[20]

From the Jefferson Street intersection, drive four blocks west along Main Street to Vine Street. Turn right and drive two blocks. Turn left on Jane Street (Highway 31) and drive 1.1 miles to Darby Lane. Turn left and drive 0.6 mile to the old home called Darby, atop a bluff on your left.

Darby*

Darby, originally known as Coteau, is one of the four homes that stood at the compass points of Spanish Lake in the early 1800s. It is certain that the home's builder was François St. Marc Darby, and it is widely held that the date of construction was 1813. Louis St. Marc Darby occupied the home in 1845, and he was followed in 1913 by Octave Darby. The house remained in the family until 1970.

During the war, Union troops rode into the home and wrecked the interior, and this useless act seemed to herald the end of the days of splendor at Darby. The old Coteau Plantation never recovered financially after the war, and the land was sold, bit by bit, until only the houseplace remained.

Darby is a two-story house built of *briquette-entre-poteau*. A second-floor gallery runs around

Adrien Persac's original painting of Darby cannot be found, but this reproduction, from an old photograph, shows the home, cistern house, garconnieres *and slave quarters. (Courtesy of Arthur Lemann Jr.)*

the front and one side of the structure, and the undersection was once floored with bricks. Two stairways, one on the front and one on the side, lead to the gallery from underneath. Six sets of columns—brick (once stuccoed) below and wood above—line the front gallery, and five line the side gallery. It is obvious that a third section of the gallery once existed on another side of the home, for today the eave of the roof protrudes unsupported on that side.

It is certain that this was never true of the fourth side, however, for Adrien Persac's painting of the home shows this quite plainly. Persac painted Darby in 1861, but the location of the original painting has been a mystery for many years. Fortunately, however, photographs of the work remain. The brick domes of two old cisterns can still be seen on one side of the home, and the Persac painting shows that these were once housed in a large outbuilding.

Darby has been roofed in tin to slow the destruction being dealt by nature. Fragments of past grandeur, however, remain. Bits of the old blocking course can still be seen here and there on the entablature, and doors and windows still bear the signs of impressive woodwork. Funds are now being raised by the Attakapas Historical

Segura was built in the 1810s and saved from ruins in the 1960s.

Society for the restoration of Darby, and it appears that the work will be done just in the nick of time. The home will be used as a museum building when restoration is complete.

On February 6, 1979, Darby burned. Plans are being made to build a replica using the remaining original walls and columns.

Continue on Darby Lane to Highway 182. Turn right and drive 0.9 mile to Segura (on the right).

Segura

Segura (private) stands on the south shore of Spanish Lake and was built by Raphael Segura around the year of 1812. Like Darby, the home was reduced to near ruins by time and neglect, but Segura was beautifully restored in the 1960s by the T. C. Holloman family. The bricks were taken apart, cleaned, and reassembled perfectly, and the wood was replaced where needed. The finished product is a beautiful old home with every advantage of a modern dwelling. Six square columns support the gallery of Segura, and a stairway climbs to the gallery from beneath. The gallery is enclosed by a wooden balustrade and six colonettes. Louvered shutters adorn the windows of the brick lower floor and of the weatherboarded upper section of the structure.

Drive 2.3 miles farther west on Highway 182 to the brick gateposts that divide the long white fence which surrounds Dulcito. A long gravel drive leads to the home.

Dulcito

Dulcito is set in an area shaded by literally hundreds of pecan, magnolia, and live oak trees near Spanish Lake. This is a one-and-one-half-story house of cypress and *bousillage*, set low to the ground on a brick foundation. Six square wooden columns line the main gallery, and a shorter gallery runs along the east side of the home. Both are now screened.

Dulcito was built in 1788, and it was used as a summer residence for its builder, Dauterieve Dubuclet. A Confederate training facility called Camp Pratt was located on Spanish Lake near Dulcito, and the home served for a time as a Confederate hospital. Its well, said to have been

Dulcito stands on the southern shore of Spanish Lake.

the deepest in the area, provided the camp with water. The old home received a thorough restoration in 1954 at the hands of the George Trappey family, and it is open for tours by appointment. Call (318) 369–3368.

Our Lady of the Lake

This once proud structure (private) stands near Dulcito on Spanish Lake, and there is no access to the home by public roads. Built by Jean Baptiste Despanet de Blanc in 1827, Our Lady of the Lake was ransacked by Federal troops during the war and was later pillaged by vandals. It has been in ruins for several years.

The one-and-one-half-story home is set on a high, many-roomed brick basement. Round brick columns support the gallery that completely surrounds the home, and slender colonettes line the gallery beneath the now dilapidated hipped roof. The basement is floored with hexagonal Spanish tiles, and the plaster walls were once painted to resemble marble (the beautiful and tedious artform called *faux marbe*). The plaster has long since fallen from the upstairs walls, revealing their crossed beams filled with mud and moss. The doorways inside and out boast handsome fanlights, unusual in that they are hinged for opening to the breeze. Of the many fireplaces, some have hand-carved mantels and others have mantels of ornate ironwork. The marble slabs that once graced the hearths have been removed.

Drive out Dulcito's gravel drive, turn left on Highway 182 (which becomes West St. Peter Street in New Iberia), and drive 5.6 miles to the Iberia Savings and Loan Association (on the left) at the corner of Weeks and St. Peter Streets. Beside this building, facing Weeks Street, is the ancient statue of Hadrian.

Statue of Hadrian

This marble statue of Hadrian was created about 130 A.D. Hadrian, emperor of Rome from 117 to 138 A.D., was a leader of justice, strength, and wisdom, and he traveled throughout the Roman Empire stabilizing government and beautifying cities with new architecture. He is perhaps best remembered for the seventy-three-mile Hadrian Wall in England and for the great walls he had built in Germany.

The statue, over seven feet tall and said to weigh more than a ton, had stood in a number of locations throughout the world before it was taken to New Orleans by a wealthy collector. It was purchased and placed here as a public service by the New Iberia Savings and Loan Associ-

Our Lady of the Lake, now in complete ruins, was painted by Adrien Persac in 1861, when the mansion was in its prime. (Courtesy of Mr. Felix Kuntz, deceased.)

ation in 1961, and it has since become a familiar sight to passers-by in the town of New Iberia.

Next door to Iberia Savings and Loan is Renoudet Cottage, at 315 East St. Peter Street.

Renoudet Cottage

The age of this home, now called Renoudet Cottage (private), is not known, but by 1840 it had come into the possession of a Picard family. It was later occupied for a time by William Weeks II (son of the builder of the Shadows), and it was used at other times to house the overseers of the Weeks family's plantations. The charming little dwelling is fronted by a short gallery with a wooden balustrade and four ornate colonettes.

Drive one block east on St. Peter and turn right on Center Street. Center will become Highway 14, and a ten-mile drive south leads to Highway 702. Turn right and drive a short distance to Jefferson Island.

LIVE OAK GARDENS

The area now called Jefferson Island, one of Louisiana's five great salt domes that rise like "islands" above the surrounding marshlands, was once owned by a man named Randolph, related by marriage to the pirate Jean Lafitte. Lafitte used the place as a hideout on several occasions, and it is said, of course, that he buried treasure on the property.

Joseph Jefferson, one of America's greatest nineteenth-century actors, purchased the property in the 1860s for a country retreat. He was responsible for the beginnings of the beautiful Rip Van Winkle's Live Oak Gardens, named for his most famous theatrical portrayal. In 1870 Jefferson built his magnificent home in the center of these extensive gardens. President Grover Cleveland, a frequent guest, was fond of relaxing beneath the branches of a particularly large and beautiful live oak that now bears his name. The Cleveland Oak stands only a few yards from the home and is a member of the Louisiana Live Oak Society.

Three trails through the gardens have been mapped out for visitors. The Camellia and Azalea Trails speak for themselves, and the Summer Trail leads through spectacular gardens of hibiscus, bougainvillea, and hundreds of other plants, many tropical. The Japanese Tea Garden is a recent and pleasant addition, and elsewhere in the gardens are memorable greenhouse displays. The gardens are open 9:00 a.m. to 5:00 p.m. daily.

Drive back out Parish Highway 702 to Highway 14. Turn left and drive 7.0 miles (crossing U.S. 90) to Highway 329. Turn right on 329, which leads (crossing U.S. 90 again) to Avery Island.

JUNGLE GARDENS

Avery Island, then called Petite Anse Island and owned by Judge Daniel D. Avery, is the site of the first rock salt deposit ever discovered in the continental United States.[21] It was the only salt supply of the Confederate Army and the Southern states during the war, and the destruction of the mining operations had long been the

This statue of Roman Emperor Hadrian is 1800 years old.

goal of Union General Nathaniel P. Banks. When General Dick Taylor withdrew from the Bayou Teche area after the Battle of Irish Bend, the Confederate troops guarding the mine were forced to evacuate also. Union forces occupied the abandoned island on April 17, 1863, and all the equipment and buildings were destroyed.[22]

Today, above Avery Island's gigantic salt dome sprawls more than two hundred acres of landscaped, cultivated beauty. The Jungle Gardens are the product of the vast fortune garnered from the cultivation of hot peppers, the manufacturing of world-famous Tabasco Sauce, the drilling of oil, and the mining of the salt deposit that lies below. This empire of natural beauty was the creation of E. A. McIlhenny, the nineteenth- and twentieth-century explorer, conservationist, naturalist, and author who followed Judge Avery as owner of the island.

McIlhenny, a great man of varied interests and abilities, was responsible for saving the nearly extinct egrets, which now number in the tens of thousands due to his efforts. He was a big game hunter whose world records still stand. He

Renoudet Cottage was built prior to 1840.

The old Joe Jefferson home on Jefferson Island might remind one of Sleeping Beauty's castle.

was an explorer who traveled virtually the entire world. As a naturalist he collected thousands of rare and exotic plants from around the world and created hundreds of new varieties of his own. He was also responsible for the introduction of nutrias to the United States—a boon to Louisiana's fur industry.

Many visitors come here each year to drive and walk the acres of fascination which is the Jungle Gardens. One special attraction is Bird City, where thousands of egret families make their homes each year. Another is the Chinese Garden, with a gigantic Buddha whose first home was a temple near Peiping around the year 1000 A.D. Visitors can see flowers and plants that they have neither seen nor heard of before, as well as new varieties of familiar plants that they have never imagined.

Return via Highway 329 to Highway 14. Turn right and follow Highway 14 (it becomes Center Street in New Iberia) until it ends on East Main Street. Turn left, drive three blocks (passing the Shadows again), and turn right on Bridge Street to cross the bayou.

From the bridge, Bridge Street (which becomes Duperier Avenue and later Highway 86) leads 3.8 miles to Justine (on the left).

JUSTINE

Eight one-story fluted Doric columns and a wooden balustrade with ornate spindles line Justine's gallery and steps. The hipped roof is broken by a huge, arched dormer window of Victorian vintage. The back section of the home was constructed in 1822, while the facade is a product of the 1890s. The house was moved by barge from Centerville to its present location in 1967.

Except for the hand-carved mantels brought from Europe in the 1890s, the woodwork throughout the home is entirely of cypress, including the curly cypress paneling. The furniture is primarily Early Victorian. Some items of special interest to visitors are a Mallard bookcase from New Orleans, a Louis XV desk that dates to 1754, the beautiful hand-carved stairway, antique crockery and ironware in the kitchen, glass cases containing Chitimacha Indian artifacts (including woven baskets over two hundred years old), a trunk purchased for a trip to Paris in the 1840s by the Duperier family of New Iberia, framed coins and bills (including half-dimes and a Louisiana five-dollar bill from the early 1800s), and a flintlock with brass inlays (which, according to the Smithsonian, predates 1720).

Next door to Justine stands a picturesque cypress building—a country store built in the 1890s, which now houses the Justine Bottle Museum. The bottles tell the story of history in a unique and most interesting way. Two-, three-, and four-hundred-year-old bottles are common in this museum, and a few are of even greater antiquity.

From Justine, drive 5.2 miles farther along Highway 86, into the town of Loreauville, to the signs (on the left) that mark the location of the Heritage Museum.

LOREAUVILLE HERITAGE MUSEUM

The Loreauville Heritage Museum is set in the acre-large backyard of the owners, Mr. and

Almost one thousand years old, this Buddha overlooks a sleepy lagoon in the heart of the Jungle Gardens of Avery Island.

Justine, built in 1822, received its Victorian facade in the 1890s.

Mrs. James J. Barras, on gently sloping land that leads down to the bayouside. As visitors walk through the outdoor museum, they walk in effect through more than three centuries of bayou history. There is first a seventeenth-century Attakapas Indian village, with artifacts from local burial grounds. (There are, in fact, two Indian mounds nearby.) Spaniards arrived in the Loreauville area in 1779, and the museum features a pioneer village based on that era. Here are wooden tools, straw hats, moss mattresses and household goods, homes built of rough-hewn cypress boards, and the corn, indigo, hemp, tobacco, cotton, flax, and wool which were the early products of this area. When the visitor arrives at the nineteenth century, he sees an Acadian farmhouse with its spinning wheels, wood-and-mud-chimneyed fireplace, furniture, clothing, and cooking apparatus. From that same century is a blacksmith shop with its tools, a voodoo shack with its *gris-gris* and its *voodooienne* leaning over some toxic brew, a Gypsy camp spread about the traditional wagon, and a livery stable with many interesting buggies and wagons.

Finally the visitor strolls through a "turn-of-the-century" village, depicting a bayou town of the early twentieth century. It includes a tiny church, barbershop, saloon, jail, cobbler's shop, dairy, post office and hardware store, and a combination pharmacy-dentist's office. Each of these is filled with the tools and goods of its particular function. Mrs. Barras explains her special attention to this era by saying that we are often too busy preserving the mementoes of the distant past to pay attention to those items of our more recent past that will soon have disappeared completely.

Leave the museum and drive 5.8 miles farther along the east bank of Bayou Teche on Highway 86. Here you will cross to the west bank, and a 0.6-mile drive on Highway 86 from the bridge will take you to Belmont.

BELMONT

Belmont (private) is fronted by a fence that is lined with much foliage. An old-fashioned stile offers access to the large yard, and a walkway leads beneath huge, ivy-covered oaks to the home. The original Belmont was constructed in 1765 for a Spanish government official. It was purchased in 1830 by H. W. Pwebles, and in 1858 it passed into the possession of his daughter, who married Confederate Major John Fletcher Wyche. U.S. General Banks used Belmont as his headquarters for a time, after Mrs. Wyche and her son John had fled to Texas to avoid the experience of Union occupation. They returned in 1865.[23] The home was destroyed by fire in 1947, but it was rebuilt by James Wright Wyche, Jr.

Six fluted Doric columns line the gallery of this one-story home, differing from the original in that the first had eight columns and dormer windows. On the bank of Bayou Teche behind Belmont are the pilings of an old steamboat wharf. The old plantation bell was cast in 1859 by the Buckeye Foundry of Cincinnati. On the viewer's right of Belmont stands a building whose central structure was the old plantation office, probably built in the 1760s. Its roofline was changed, and major additions were made in the 1970s when it was converted to a residence.

Drive 0.4 mile farther along Highway 86 to Highway 31. Turn right, and it is 2.7 miles to Keystone Oaks (on the left).

The manor of Keystone Oaks, which stood at the end of this oak alley until it burned, has been replaced by the old plantation overseer's house.

KEYSTONE OAKS

Keystone Oaks (private) stands at the end of a double row of live oaks. There are fourteen trees in the avenue and a total of twenty-five great oaks in the large yard. On one side of the home is a double row of pecan trees. The trees are all quite large, the largest oak measuring over one hundred feet in limbspan. The manor of the plantation called Keystone Oaks was destroyed by fire more than sixty-five years ago. The present structure is the old overseer's home, which was moved to the spot at the end of the oak alley after the fire. The plantation's name can be attributed to the fact that its first owner had been a native of Pennsylvania, the Keystone State.

The old overseer's home, with its hipped roof, is a two-story structure fronted by a single gallery and four small Doric columns. A widow's walk lines the eaves above the gallery. The ruins of the plantation's old sugar refinery may be found just across Highway 31 from the home.

Drive 1.7 miles farther north on Highway 31 to the Old Labbe House, on the right.

OLD LABBE HOUSE

The Old Labbe House (private) is a two-story home with a long single gallery. The gallery, shaded by modern awning, is lined by six short columns set on high brick pedestals, and three large dormers can be seen above. This was once a three-story home, but when the bricks of the lower floor began to crumble, the building was jacked up, the lower floor was removed, and the remaining portion was lowered. The inner walls are of mud and moss, while the outer walls are of brick covered with weatherboards.

Eugene Duchamp de Chastagnier imigrated to Bayou Teche from the West Indies in the mid-1800s. He built this home for his daughter, whose son, T. J. Labbe, later became a state senator. Duchamp's own townhouse in St. Martinville and plantation home are among the favorite attractions of this area.

Drive 1.2 miles farther on Highway 31 (it will become South Main Street in St. Martinville) to Gary Street.

Turn right and drive to the end of the street. On the left stands the house numbered 223.

ST. MARTINVILLE AREA

The Bell Telephone sign, *Compagnie de Télé-phone Bell du Centre-Sud*, on the main street of this historic town, reassures you that St. Martin-ville is the heart of French Louisiana. The first permanent settlement of the entire Teche re-gion was established here in 1760 by Gabriel Fuselier de la Claire. A military garrison, *Poste des Attakapas*, was established, and the village was known by that name until 1812. Acadian ref-ugees began arriving in the mid-1760s, fol-lowed by an inflow of Royalists fleeing the dan-gers of the French Revolution and of planters forced to evacuate their West Indies plantations due to slave revolts.

These wealthy French families brought to St. Martinville the grand balls, the gala weddings, the opera, and the finery to which they had been accustomed elsewhere, and the town became known as *la Petite Paris*.[24] The great number of aristocrats from those sources, in fact, has caused the language spoken here even today to be much nearer pure French than the Acadian (Cajun) French spoken throughout the rest of the Bayou Country. It is now believed, however, that Cajun French is not a corruption of the language, but rather the preservation of the French language as it existed when those sturdy French pioneers first colonized Acadia (today's Nova Scotia). Their isolation prevented the natural evolution of language that occurs in larger societies. (A similar situation exists in the Ozark Mountains. Isolated pockets of people there speak not corrupt English, as it was long regarded, but near perfect Old English.)

223 Gary Street

This fine raised cottage (private) was con-structed early in the nineteenth century by Dr. Alexandre Landry, who remained the owner until 1821. During the war, the home served as quarters for Union officers. A fire in 1913 dam-aged the cypress shingles of the roof; and in 1927, the year of the great Mississippi River

The old home at 223 Gary Street in St. Martinville has withstood fire and flood.

flood, the home was under water for three weeks. (These were hard times, of course, but the children had great fun riding *pirogues* through the rooms and in and out of the doors of their home.)

Built of bricks below and weatherboards above, this two-and-one-half-story home is fronted by a brick porch, level with the ground, and an upper gallery that is lined with colonettes and a wooden balustrade. Red board shutters with their original hardware adorn the windows and double doors below, and shuttered windows flank the main doorway above. The brick col-umns that once supported the upper gallery have been replaced by chamfered wooden posts. The exposed beams of the gallery's ceiling boast handcut beading.

The interior walls are of *briquette entre poteaux* construction (brick between beams). The hand-carved mantels, as well as the transomed doors with their brass fixtures in the central hall-way and throughout the home, are original. Large armoires, one mantel of Italian marble, tester beds, and other fine antiques add charm

The St. Martin Courthouse was constructed in 1853.

to the already lovely home. The shady side yard leads down to Bayou Teche.

Return to Main Street, turn right, and drive one block to the courthouse (at the corner of Main and Berard).

St. Martin Courthouse

Four massive, fluted Ionic columns support the heavy entablature of the St. Martin Parish Courthouse. It was constructed in 1853, and its facade has remained unchanged, though the structure was enlarged in 1917. A dentil course adorns the entablature, and an unusual round window is set into the center of the pediment. More of the large Ionics may be seen on the sides of the building.

The old records housed here are a treasure of information, and some of the papers date to 1760. An early judge who served in this building was Edward Simon, who is credited with telling the story of Evangeline to Nathaniel Hawthorne while they were both at Harvard. Hawthorne in turn told it to Henry Wadsworth Longfellow. Simon's son, grandson, and great-grandson followed him as judges of St. Martin Parish.

From the courthouse at the corner of Main and Berard, drive one block west on Berard to the house numbered 201 (on the left).

201 Berard

This house (private) was constructed in 1849 by William Eastin. Eight square columns (two

The home at 201 Berard Street in St. Martinville was built in 1849.

engaged) line the gallery of the weatherboarded home, and three dormer windows are set into the gable roof. The entablature and the capitals of the columns are ornamented with dentil courses, and the handsome doorway is enhanced by a transom and sidelights. The gallery is enclosed by a balustrade of latticework.

Drive two blocks farther along Berard Street to College Street. Turn right and drive two blocks to the home at 218 College.

218 College

This weatherboarded house (private) once stood next to the Old Labbe House, but it was moved to this location by oxen years ago. Three (count 'em) fluted Ionic columns rise two stories from the single gallery to support the eaves of the hipped roof. A balcony with an ornate wooden balustrade spans nearly the entire

width of the facade. Red Spanish tile covers the roof and the single dormer window.

Drive one block farther on College Street to Port Street. Turn right and drive three blocks to Main Street. In the southwest corner of this intersection, facing Main Street, is the Bienvenu Brothers Clothing Store.

Old Opera House

The ancient building that now houses the Bienvenu Brothers Clothing Store once housed the theater where wealthy planters took their families to see performances by traveling opera companies. St. Martinville, like New Orleans, enjoyed opera long before New York City. In a diary that was later incorporated into a book by George Washington Cable, the opera house was mentioned as having been seen by a visitor as early as 1795.[25]

Later the structure served as headquarters of the local vigilantes group that struggled to maintain justice in the corrupt years of Reconstruction.

The old opera house was owned for a time by Eugene Duchamp. His townhouse stands just across the street, and his plantation home is just west of St. Martinville. On the front and side of the opera house are spots where the bricks are of a lighter-than-usual shade. These mark the places where windows and balconies were originally located.

Duchamp Townhouse

Just across Main Street from the old opera house in St. Martinville is the old townhouse of Eugene Duchamp de Chastagnier, said to be a near replica of his former plantation home in Martinique. Each level of the pedimented portico is enclosed by an attractive wrought-iron balustrade, made in New Orleans especially for this home. Duchamp's architect was David Sandoz, and the home was completed in 1876. It served as St. Martinville's post office from 1939 until recently. Four square columns front the building, and the capitals are ornamented with blocking courses. An arched, louvered window

may be seen in the center of the pediment, and a large cupola is set into the main section of the roof.

St. Martin's Church faces Main Street in the first block past Duchamp's townhouse.

St. Martin's Church

St. Martin of Tours Catholic Church, completed in 1832, incorporated the village's first chapel, which had been built in 1765 or shortly thereafter. The first resident priest was Father Jean François, a Capuchin, who arrived in 1765.

The steeple contains three bells. The smallest, christened Auguste, rings one hour before

St. Martin de Tours dates to 1832. Its old box pews remain.

St. Martin's rectory was constructed in 1858.

High Mass every Sunday and is named for an early parish priest, Pere Auguste Thebault, who is buried in the church. The second bell, Stéphanie, has a deeper tone and rings a half-hour before mass. The largest bell, Angeli, weighs 2,100 pounds and joins the other two in sounding the final call.

Upon entering the massive doors with their original box locks and hinges, a visitor notices that the traditional Stations of the Cross are statues. Fourteen large Doric columns soar from their pedestals to the ceiling. Above the beautiful altar is a huge painting of St. Martin of Tours, painted in the 1830s by Jean François Mouchet.

Above one of the side altars is a replica of the Grotto of Lourdes, made of mud and plaster by an early member of the parish. Hanging here and there about the shrine are small marble slabs with brief thank-you notes to Mary for favors granted. Some of the *mercis* date to the late 1880s. It is said that the ornate marble baptismal font was a gift to the parish from King Louis XVI, who met his demise before it arrived in St. Martinville. (Its elaborate lid was made locally.) The church's original box pews have been flawlessly preserved. The rear of the old church consists of a single turret, onto which is set a handsome cupola of white wood.

Petite Paris Museum

Next door to St. Martin's Church is the old Knights of Columbus Hall, which now houses the Petite Paris Museum. This two-story building is fronted with four square columns, and these support the gallery and simple pediment. Shuttered windows and transomed, sidelighted doors may be seen on each level. The second-floor door is fanlighted.

The old structure, built in 1861 some seven blocks away, first housed Attakapas College, founded by Professor J. Alcee Judice. Pulled by (some say) one hundred oxen, it was rolled on logs to its present location in 1883, where it became the Knights of Columbus Hall. It has housed the museum since the early 1970s. In front of the building stands a statue of an Attakapas Indian, honoring the tribe that roamed the Teche Country long before the first Frenchmen arrived.

The Rectory

On the opposite side of St. Martin's Church from the Petite Paris Museum stands the parish rectory (private). This beautiful building was constructed about 1858. Set on pedestals, six fluted Doric columns line the two galleries and support the handsome entablature. The upper gallery is enclosed by an elegant white balustrade.

Evangeline Statue

In 1713 France deeded Acadia (present-day Nova Scotia) to England. In 1755, as war neared between France and England, the British demanded that the Acadians swear allegiance and denounce their Roman Catholic faith. The story of the forced exodus that occurred when they refused is known by every schoolchild in Louisiana. In the hasty evacuation, Louis Arceneaux was separated from his fiancée, Emmeline Labiche. Emmeline reached St. Martinville three years after Louis and found that he, thinking her lost forever, had married another. Emmeline lived for a few months with the Widow Borda and died, tradition has it, of a broken heart. At least the basic facts of this story are true, and the grave of Emmeline Labiche can be seen today in the tiny cemetery beside St. Martin's Church. Arceneaux settled near the town of Carencro in 1787, and his old home still stands.

This is the story that was made famous by the pen of Henry Wadsworth Longfellow, who named his characters Gabriel and Evangeline. In 1929, the story was made into a motion picture called *The Romance of Evangeline*, and it was filmed in St. Martinville. The cast and crew of the silent movie presented a statue of Evangeline to the town. Dolores del Rio, who played the title role, was the model for the statue which today stands over the grave of Emmeline Labiche.

From Main Street, drive down Port Street (between the Duchamp townhouse and the church square) to Bayou Teche. At the end of the street stands the Evangeline Oak.

Evangeline Oak

Easily the most famous member of the Louisiana Live Oak Society, the Evangeline Oak stands on the west bank of Bayou Teche in St. Martinville as it has for more than two hundred years. Tradition has it that Emmeline Labiche (Evangeline) landed beneath this tree, after her long journey from Acadia, to find her lover already married. It is a reasonable belief, for this would have been the logical landing place, in the heart of the village, for anyone traveling to St. Martinville by boat.

Old Castillo Hotel

Beside Bayou Teche and almost beneath the branches of the Evangeline Oak stands Mercy High School. Pilasters support the simulated balcony over the main entrance, with its fanlight and sidelights. Three dormer windows are set into the gable roof, and the color of the bricks bespeaks the building's age.

The old building was built circa 1835 by Jean Pierre Vasseur, and it served for a time as his residence. It is a two-story structure of brick and pegged cypress, and there were originally front and rear galleries. By 1840 Vasseur had opened the Union Ballroom (*Salle de l'Union*) in his home, and meals were served in his "grand hall." Charles Dutel purchased the hotel in 1843, and it was later purchased and operated by Don Louis Broussard from 1850 through 1858. From 1858–1876 it was known as *Maison des Allemands*, and it was owned during that period by the brothers Anton and Wilhelm Hesse. The hotel changed hands again in 1876, and Madame Edmond Castillo (widow of a

The old Castillo Hotel has housed a Catholic school for many years.

steamboat captain) managed the concern for the new owners until her death in 1899. The building was purchased that year by the Sisters of Mercy (who had arrived in St. Martinville in 1881), and it still houses Mercy High School.

Return to Main Street and turn right. It is several blocks to the entrance (on the right) of the Longfellow-Evangeline State Commemorative Area.

Longfellow-Evangeline State Commemorative Area

The Longfellow-Evangeline State Commemorative Area consists of 157 acres of the beautiful natural landscaping for which the banks of Bayou Teche are famous. Huge old live oaks and cypress trees make the park perpetually shady.

Just inside the gates is the Acadian Crafts House, which contains many items of Acadian handicrafts, gifts, and souvenirs. The building itself is not old, but it is reminiscent of South Louisiana's traditional "Cajun cabins," which still stand in great numbers. Strictly speaking, these are Caribbean-Creole houses, brought to Louisiana by other immigrants and quickly adopted by the Acadians.[26] The true folk house of Acadia (of which few examples remain in Louisiana) lacked a porch. The chimney, made of mud packed into a cypress frame, as seen at the crafts house, is fairly common and may have been a Canadian influence, though the typical Caribbean-Creole cottages had inside chimneys.

From the crafts house visitors follow the winding road through the park to the museum. Near the parking area is a monument honoring Judge Felix Voorhies, a man whose memory is beloved in the Bayou Country. In his public life he was a lawyer, legislator, and jurist. As a literary figure he produced short stories, contributed to the leading journals of France and Canada, edited the St. Martinville *Observer*, wrote and produced plays and musical comedies, and authored *Acadian Reminiscences* (which recounts the expulsion of the Acadians from Nova Scotia and offers a comparison of the true and fictionalized stories of Evangeline).

Outside the museum are *pirogues* and other items of interest. A replica of the old kitchen stands behind the home on its original foundations, and a replica of the old storehouse now contains restrooms. The museum itself, a Creole raised cottage, was probably built in 1765 by Chevalier M. D'Hauterive. A later owner of the property, however, was the widow of Chevalier Paul Augustin le Pelletier de la Houssaye (commandant of a French military post in Arkansas before taking command of the *Poste des Attakapas* for the Spanish), and she is known to have built a new home somewhere on the property several years prior to her death in 1784. The museum could possibly be that home. The building has been refurnished authentically, and it reflects the life-style of the wealthier settlers of the Teche region in that early day.

On the front lawn is a live oak of astounding size and beauty—a member of the Louisiana Live Oak Society called the Gabriel Oak. From beneath its branches visitors can enjoy a splendid view of the old end-gabled raised cottage. Six brick columns support the gallery, with its wooden balustrade and six wooden columns. The lower floor is constructed of brick, and the upper is of mud-and-moss covered with weatherboards. Portions of the rear galleries were converted into additional rooms in 1815. The building was restored in 1976.

Leave the park and turn left on West Main Street (Highway 31). Drive back to the heart of St. Martinville and turn right on Port Street (Highway 96). From that intersection it is 4.2 miles to Duchamp (on the left).

This famous old Creole raised cottage, located on the grounds of the Longfellow-Evangeline State Commemorative Area, now contains the Acadian House Museum.

Duchamp

Eugene Duchamp de Chastagnier arrived in the St. Martinville area before 1850. He had traveled from Martinique in the West Indies, and this is the home (private) he built on his new plantation prior to building his townhouse in St. Martinville.

Duchamp was constructed in the mid-1800s. Eight square, plaster-covered brick columns support its gallery. A green-trimmed white balustrade connects the eight colonettes that support the eave of the roof beneath the three dormer windows. Three chimneys are visible at the peak of the roof, and it appears that there was once another. The home is situated atop a grassy hill that sweeps down to the highway. Not visible from the highway is the home's rear gallery, one end of which has been enclosed in recent years.

> Turn around at Duchamp and drive 1.0 mile back on Highway 96 to the intersection of an unmarked road. Turn right, and the first house on the left is the old overseer's house of Duchamp Plantation.

Duchamp Overseer's House

This small raised cottage (private) was constructed in the mid-1800s to serve as the home for the Duchamp Plantation overseer, and it has continued to serve that purpose to this day (1978). A balustrade connects the six wooden columns that line the single gallery. The transoms and sidelights of the doorways and the hand-carved spindles and railing of the balustrade make the old house a handsome and interesting landmark.

> Turn around at the overseer's house and drive back to the stop sign at Highway 96. From the sign, it is 3.2 miles on Highway 96 back to Main Street in St. Martinville. Turn left on Main, drive one block, and turn right on Bridge Street. Drive two blocks to the small brick home (on the left) numbered 221 (which is directly across Bridge Street from a small convenience store).

The Sunday House

It was once customary for wealthy planters to build "Sunday houses" (*maisons du Dimanche*) for the purpose of having a place to relax before Mass, after their long ride into town from the country, and for entertaining friends after the service. It is believed that this home was built for that purpose and that it is the only remaining Sunday house in St. Martinville.

It was built of cypress and *bousillage* by Gabriel Bouillet in 1815, and it was restored in 1976 by Mr. and Mrs. Stanley Stockstill.[27] Four square columns line the single gallery and support the eave of the shingled gable roof. Legend has it

Duchamp was built by Eugene Duchamp de Chastagnier in the mid-1800s.

that one resident of the home during its many years of existence was a beautiful octaroon named Madeline, a niece of the famous New Orleans *voodooienne*, Marie Laveau. It is said that Madeline also practiced the ancient art of voodoo.

Cross the Bayou Teche bridge, and drive to the house (on the left) numbered 517 East Bridge Street (at the corner of Cemetery Street).

517 East Bridge

This one-and-one-half-story building (private) is fronted by four short columns on high pedestals, and it is now roofed in tin. St. Martinville folk tell a story involving the size of the house. It was originally intended to be a two-story home with attic, they say, and shortly before the War Between the States the bricks and lumber were assembled for the task. Then came the war years, and construction was delayed for the duration. Building materials ran short in the little town with most of the labor force off at war, and the materials for this house were cheerfully given to neighbors in need. When the war ended and construction was ready to begin, there was only enough material left for the small home that stands here today. It was completed in the late 1860s.

Turn right on Cemetery Street and right again on Cora. Drive down to the bayou, and turn left on the tiny boulevard. Just past the first house on the left is a brick walkway that disappears into the vegetation at 311 Olivier Boulevard.

Monsieur André Olivier

This is the home (private) of M. André Olivier (1978), and it was built before the War Between the States. (M. André's brother was born here in 1870.) The two-story cottage is fronted by a single gallery with four wooden columns. The house was moved back from the bayou during the flood of 1927, but not in time to save the mud-and-moss mixture of the original walls. This has been replaced by weatherboards, but the watermarks can still be seen partway up the front door.

M. André is a great-grandson of the young heroine of a story, well-known to lovers of Louisiana literature, which dates to 1795. The girl was Mme. Françoise Bossier, daughter of a St. James Parish plantation owner. The story is called "The Adventures of Françoise and Suzanne," and it is one of George Washington Cable's *Strange True Stories of Louisiana*, published in 1889.[28] The story recounts a trip through the beautiful Atchafalaya and Teche region to St. Martinville.

M. André has made the study of Acadian history and the collection of historic pictures, items, and documents on that subject his life's work. His collection may be seen in his museum on East Bridge Street.

Continue along Olivier Boulevard, which curves to intersect with Cemetery Street. Turn left on Cemetery and right on East Bridge Street. It is 1.0 mile on East Bridge (Highway 96) to Oak and Pine Alley.

OAK AND PINE ALLEY

This magnificent double row of oak and pine trees leads from Highway 96 to the spot where Pine Alley Plantation house once stood. The home was built and the alleyway planted by Charles Durand, who arrived from France in 1820. Durand planted crossing alleys of the trees, originally three miles long, that stretched from his home to Bayou Teche. A double-eye hurricane in 1947 destroyed almost two miles of the major alley and completely uprooted the shorter section. Roughly a mile and a quarter remains of the alley.

Durand's daughters were married at a double ceremony at his plantation on May 21, 1870, and the gala event is one of the best-known stories of Louisiana lore. Spiders were brought from Catahoula Lake, according to the story, and turned loose in the three-mile alley to weave webs between the trees and across the roadway. Bellows were then used to shower the dew-moistened webs with gold dust, beneath which the wedding party drove. Where was Matthew Brady when we needed him?

From Oak and Pine Alley, drive 2.5 miles farther along Highway 96 to Les Memoires.

The delightful plantation home called Les Memoires *was built in 1834.*

LES MEMOIRES

Les Memoires (private) was built by Aldelard de Rouselle in 1836, and it was restored in the 1960s by Mr. and Mrs. Merkel Stuckey. The large yard, with its four hundred azaleas and camellias, is enclosed by a picket fence. The old plantation bell is mounted between two lamp-posts and near an old and gigantic sugar kettle.

Six brick and plaster columns support the gallery of this two-and-one-half-story structure. The gallery is lined with six square, wooden columns which are connected by an ornate wooden balustrade. Louvered shutters may be seen on each level of the facade, and a Greek key course (an unusual touch in Louisiana) ornaments the entablature. Two dormer windows and a large chimney are set into the gabled roof. One side of the home has a pleasant little balcony.

Les Memoires was once set on high brick foundations, but the undersection was enclosed long ago to form today's lower floor. The interior and exterior walls are sixteen inches thick. The lower floor is brick, and behind the weatherboards of the upper floor are walls built of a mixture of mud, oyster shells, and lime.

Turn around at Les Memoires and drive 0.6 mile back on Highway 96 to St. John Road. Turn right and drive 1.5 miles to Highway 347, which follows the east bank of Bayou Teche. Turn left on 347 and drive 0.1 mile to St. John.

ST. JOHN

St. John Plantation (private) was once known as Lizima. The manor was constructed in 1828 by Alexandre Etienne de Clouet, and he named it for his daughter, Marie Lizima de Clouet. Alexandre was Louisiana's representative to the

Confederate government in the early days of secession, and he was a descendant of Chevalier Alexandre de Clouet, first commandant of the *Poste des Attakapas*.

Shortly after his home was built, Alexandre took a large Indian basket and went about gathering seedlings of oak, pine, and magnolia. These he planted in rows, along with fruit trees, in his large front yard. By 1861 the trees were quite large, as can be seen in the painting of the home executed that year by Adrien Persac. It is said that when De Clouet lost his home in the 1880s, the grief-stricken old man embraced every tree before leaving. The fine groves of trees—two inner rows of pines flanked by two rows of magnolias, flanked in turn by the rows of live oaks—was largely destroyed in the disastrous hurricane of 1947, though many fine oak and fruit trees still stand in the side yards.

St. John is fronted by two galleries which are lined with attractive balustrades and four Corinthian columns. A belvedere, destroyed in the hurricane and replaced, can be seen atop the hipped roof. Screening and awning have been added to the lower gallery. Two attached *garçonnières* flank the rear of the home, and the old kitchen wing is separated from the main structure by a breezeway. The home's interior boasts marble mantels and fine old plaster medallions. St. John has been flawlessly preserved by the

Beautiful St. John was constructed in 1828. (Photography in cooperation with Levert-St. John, Inc.)

Adrien Persac painted St. John in 1861, and the work quite clearly shows the fine grove of trees, planted by the builder, that was partially destroyed by the hurricane of 1947. (Courtesy of Mr. and Mrs. Frederick Nehrbass of Lafayette.)

constant and painstaking care of Levert-St. John, Inc.

Turn around at St. John and drive 10.6 miles up the east bank of Bayou Teche (through the town of Parks) on La. 347 to the home (on the right) at 625 Poydras Street in Breaux Bridge.

BREAUX BRIDGE

The Breaux Bridge area was inhabited prior to 1800 by scattered Acadian families. The townsite is at the head of what was the commercially navigable portion of Bayou Teche, so the spot grew quickly in importance. Agricolé Breaux built a bridge here in 1850, replacing an earlier toll ferry, and the name of the town was born. The village was incorporated in 1859. Breaux Bridge is the "crawfish capital of the world," and the famous Louisiana Crawfish Festival occurs here every even-numbered year in May.

625 Poydras Street

This single-story house (private) is fronted by a gallery with a balustrade and turned colonettes. Valery Pierre Thibodeaux built or purchased the home in the 1850s, and it was then a *bousillage* "shotgun" house—three rooms deep with a large shed room attached to the rear. Thibodeaux owned his own sawmill, and he expanded the home to its present configuration

The old Penn home near Breaux Bridge, recently moved here and restored, was built circa 1830 near Jeanerette.

Huron, originally called Stephanie, was built prior to 1822.

in the early 1870s. This is now (1978) the home of Thibodeaux's granddaughter, Mrs. Jean Castille, who remembers stories of Union troops camping in the yard, and of money and valuables being hidden in the days when slave insurrections were feared.

Old Penn Home

This fine old cottage (private), now located west of Breaux Bridge but not accessible by public roads, originally stood near the town of Jeanerette. It was moved to its present location in 1973 by Robert E. Smith, the young architect who is now (1978) in the midst of restoring it.

It is believed that the home was built shortly after 1830 by one Henry Penn, whose father had previously owned the land on which it was constructed. Eight turned colonettes and a wooden balustrade line the single gallery, and a stairway leads to the attic from one end. Double doors with transom and sidelights open from the gallery to the central room, and a single door provides gallery access to each of the two other front rooms. There are two rear rooms, and double doors open onto a small rear gallery.

Connected to this is a small kitchen wing (not original).

The exterior walls of *briquette-entre-poteau* are covered with the home's original beaded weatherboards, and the old cypress floors are intact. The original wooden mantels still remain— once shortened by a previous owner (adapting to coal-burning fireplaces) but now repaired. The interiors of the front rooms have been returned to their original colors. The ceilings and beaded beams are blue, the doors and chair rails are green, baseboards are gray, and mantels are black.

From 625 Poydras Street in Breaux Bridge, drive 0.2 mile farther up La. 347 (Poydras) to Grand Point Street (La. 347). Turn right and drive 6.6 miles (passing through the town of Henderson with its many seafood restaurants) to a point where La. 347 turns left. Follow 347 and drive 2.3 miles to the point where the highway turns right again. Follow Highway 347 for 2.1 miles farther to Huron (on the left).

HURON

Huron (private) was built prior to 1822, probably by Charles Lastrapes of an old Creole family of the region. The plantation was known as

Stephanie until 1835. The home is a two-and-one-half-story, end-gabled raised cottage. Soldier courses adorn the windows of the brick lower floor, and heavy, double-hinged shutters may be found on windows and French doors throughout the home. The walls of the upper floors are of *briquette-entre-poteau*. Six square brick columns support the gallery, which is lined with six colonettes and enclosed by a wooden balustrade. Two dormer windows may be seen above, and two more open to the rear.

Behind the home, the eighteen-inch brick wall is interrupted in the center by a magnificent, arched carriage entrance. The beautiful arch is partially enclosed by the base of a three-story stairway that appears to have been added many years ago, possibly when a front stairway was removed. Inside Huron—all original—are the old beaded beams, wooden "wrap-around" mantels, and wide cypress baseboards.

From Huron, drive 4.3 miles farther up La. 347 to Fuselier Street in Arnaudville. Turn left and drive three blocks on Fuselier to Market Street (La. 31), just on the near side of the Bayou Teche bridge. Turn right and drive 3.5 miles on La. 31 to Robin.

ROBIN PLANTATION

General Napoleon Robin of the French army, after Napoleon Bonaparte's exile, came to America and settled in St. Louis. He soon moved to the Leonville area, and François, one of Napoleon Robin's five sons, is said to have been the first surgeon in what is now St. Landry Parish. He was the official doctor for the *Poste des Opelousas*. The old Robin plantation home (private) is believed to have been built about 1830 by Numa Robin, son of François.[29]

The home, restored by Senator Edgar G. Mouton, Jr., of Lafayette, stands on three-foot brick foundations in the center of a circle of large live oaks. Six square columns and a wooden balustrade line the single gallery, and three dormer windows are set into the end-

Robin, built about 1830, is set in a circle of live oaks.

gabled tin roof. A front door opens from the gallery into each of the three front rooms, and a small upstairs door (exterior) provides access to an attic storage area above the gallery. Louvered shutters protect all exterior windows. There are two interior chimneys—one at the end and one near the center of the roof.

From Robin, drive 0.9 mile farther up the east bank of the Teche on La. 31, and turn left to cross the bayou bridge in Leonville. From the turn, drive 0.2 mile through downtown Leonville, and turn right again on La. 31. From that intersection it is 0.2 mile on La. 31 to the first LeMelle home (on the right, facing the highway from beyond a small field), and it is then 0.1 mile farther to the second LeMelle home (hard by the highway on the right).

LeMELLE HOMES

Both of the old LeMelle family homes (private) of Leonville were built near the close of the eighteenth century by free men of color. They are both of *bousillage* construction, weatherboarded, and both are sturdy but in a state of disrepair.[30]

The first of these, the LeMelle-Frilot home, faces Highway 31 from beyond a field on the east side of the highway. It is sheltered by a massive live oak, whose great limbs are now threatening the rear of the home. The floor of the single gallery is gone now, but the four colonettes and the steep stairway to the attic entrance have been extended to the ground. An ancient barn still stands intact behind the abandoned home.

The second LeMelle home is an end-gabled cottage with a small portico, whose floor has been dismantled. A tiny stairway leads from a rear room to a small and unusual landing, on which the climber would stand to step through an opening into the small sleeping chamber of the attic.

Famous Chretien Point was saved by the sign of the Masons.

Opelousas to Abbeville

The many colonial and antebellum homes of Opelousas itself will be covered in the third book of this series, which will be entitled *Plantation Homes of the Cotton Country*.

From the second of the two old LeMelle family homes of Leonville, drive 6.6 miles farther north on Highway 31 to the point where the highway turns left. From this point, follow Highway 31 west for 1.4 miles to U.S. 167. Turn right on 167 and drive a short distance to U.S. 190 at Opelousas. Turn left on 190 (Landry Street), and drive 1.0 mile to the intersection of Main Street. Turn left on Main (Highway 182) and drive 8.1 miles south to Highway 754. Turn right on 754 and drive 0.15 mile to an unmarked asphalt road that leads away to the left. Turn left on the unmarked road, which will fork after only a few feet. Take the right fork and drive 1.8 miles to Chretien Point.

CHRETIEN POINT

The lands of this plantation, near the village of Sunset, were granted by the Spanish government to Louis St. Germain in 1776, and Joseph Chretien acquired the property in 1781. His son Hypolyte inherited the plantation, and the present home was begun in 1831 by Hypolyte II. The builder was Samuel Young (who later constructed a portion of the old Academy of the Sacred Heart in Grand Coteau), and he was assisted by bricklayer Johnathan Harris. Hypolyte II and one of his sons died some two years later of yellow fever, leaving the estate and manor to Madame Chretien and young Hypolyte III.

Hypolyte Chretien III was the owner of the home during the years of the War Between the States. After the Battle of Vermilionville in 1863 and shortly before the Battle of Bayou Bourbeaux, Union forces under General Nathaniel Banks and Confederates commanded by General Alfred Mouton met and fought on the lands of Chretien Point. Hypolyte III, watching from his upper gallery, at one point found himself and his home in the line of fire, and by impulse he gave the Masonic distress signal. General Banks responded, called a brief cease-fire, and moved his battle line a safe distance from the home. That, however, was the limit of the general's kindness. The Union force camped on the plantation grounds for three days. They destroyed fences, the kitchen, and other outbuildings, burned crops, and killed or confiscated all livestock. (An October, 1863, edition of *Leslie's Illustrated Weekly* carried a sketch of Chretien Point, showing Union soldiers blasting away from the front yard.) Captain Florian O. Cornay, an ancestor of the present (1978) owner of Chretien Point, fought here with General Mouton. Mouton died at the Battle of Mansfield in northwest Louisiana, and Cornay died days later on the trail of the retreating Union forces. The captain's own home near Calumet had already been burned by Banks, after the Battle of Bisland.

Six plastered-brick columns, set on short, separate pedestals, rise two stories to support the eave of the hipped roof of Chretien Point. A wooden balustrade lines the second-floor gallery, and the floor of the undersection is of bricks laid in the herringbone design. That design is repeated on the brick walkways that encircle the home and on a brick patio that surrounds the home's original well. Three fan-lighted doors, paneled and beaded, provide access to the three front rooms of each level of the home. Two front windows, also arched, open onto each level, and these are protected by arched, louvered shutters. The original cypress wainscoting may still be seen along the wall of the upper gallery.

The mantels throughout the home, all original, are beautiful and unusual, and those of the second floor feature miniature Doric and Ionic columns of marble. Also to be found inside are the old *faux-bois* baseboards and a stairway which served as a model for that of Tara in one of the film versions of *Gone with the Wind*. According to the original plans that are on file in the St. Landry Parish Courthouse in Opelousas, another stairway once led to the upper gallery from beneath.

Restoration of Chretien Point was begun in 1975 by Mr. and Mrs. Louis J. Cornay. The plasterwork has been repaired, rooms have been repainted in their original colors, and one weakened column has been strengthened. The old metal roof, which had protected the home for many years, has been replaced by wooden shingles, so the home now appears just as it did when Chretien Point was fresh and new in 1832. The manor is open by appointment for tours by groups of twenty-five or more, and those interested should call (318) 234–7835 in Sunset or (318) 233–7050 in Lafayette.

Turn around at Chretien Point and return to La. 754. Turn right and drive 0.15 mile to La. 182. Turn right and drive 1.9 miles on 182 to the intersection of Duffy Avenue (La. 93) in Sunset. Turn left on La. 93, cross U.S. 167, and drive another 0.5 mile on La. 93 to the intersection of Burleigh Street in Grand Coteau. Turn left onto a driveway that leads from the Burleigh intersection to the old Duffy-Ogé home.

GRAND COTEAU

"Grand Coteau" is an exaggeration, for the town has not a single hill (*coteau*), and the ridge on which it is situated is only slightly elevated above the surrounding flatlands. The Charles Smith family, local plantation owners, provided land for St. Charles Church, for the Convent and Academy of the Sacred Heart founded here in 1821, and for St. Charles College which was founded two years later. The village has grown up around those establishments.[31]

Duffy-Ogé Home

Six square columns line the single gallery of this all-cypress home (private), and the front door, with its transom and sidelights, boasts a handsome facing, as do the windows and major interior doors of the first floor.

There are three front rooms, and two minor rear rooms flank a central dining room that may once have been a rear loggia (which would have made the home conform to the typical Creole floor plan of that era). Further evidence is that the dining room and kitchen were in a separate building when the home was constructed. The original stairway leads from the present dining room to a large room upstairs, which was intended for living quarters but never finished. The exposed beams of the attic provide evidence that the home once received a new roof. A small, original door in the base of the staircase opens onto the old herb cellar. Today's kitchen is located in a rear gallery that was added at some time and later enclosed.

The cottage was constructed by the Duffy family circa 1850. It was later owned by the Duffy's adopted son, and still later by his son,

Carlton Ogé, who lived here until his death. It was occupied by Carlton's widow until 1978. The home was purchased that year by Mr. and Mrs. Jay Smith, who will restore it.

From the driveway of the Duffy-Ogé home, turn right on Burleigh and drive 0.4 mile to the drive on the left that leads to the Burleigh home.

Burleigh Home

Robert Burleigh and two brothers arrived in America from England late in the eighteenth century, and they settled in Grand Coteau in 1798. Robert purchased his land that year, and his home (private) was probably completed in the first decade of the new century. The home is now occupied (1978) by Mr. and Mrs. Richard Burleigh—the fifth generation of that family to live here.

Two doors open onto the single gallery, with its five turned colonettes. The original stairway from gallery to attic is now gone. The old home is set on three-foot brick foundations, and it is constructed of *bousillage* and pegged cypress beams. An interior chimney is located on one end of the gabled roof. The three front rooms and two rear rooms boast their original cypress baseboards, and an old rear gallery has been enclosed.

From the driveway of the Burleigh home, turn right on Burleigh and drive 0.4 mile to Chatrian Street. Turn right, and the first home on the left that faces the street is old Sanvol-Smith home.

Sanvol-Smith Home

Six square columns line the single gallery of the old Sanvol-Smith home (private), which is set on two-foot brick foundations. Two doors serve the gallery, with its wooden balustrade, and the windows are protected by louvered shutters. Two exterior chimneys flank the end-gabled roof.

Edwin Smith, a descendant of Charles Smith, purchased this home in the first decade of this century, and it had been owned in the latter part of the nineteenth century by Gottleib Sanvol. The builder and date of construction are un-

The old Duffy-Oge home in Grand Coteau.

The old Burleigh home, perhaps Grand Coteau's oldest, has remained in its original family.

known, and the home is still (1978) a Smith family possession.

Drive farther down Chatrian Street to the end of the block. On the right, in the near corner of the Pine Street intersection, stands another Smith family residence.

Polliangue-Smith Home

The older section of this house (on the viewer's left) is perhaps 150 years old, and its builder is unknown. The newer portion was constructed circa 1873 by Maurice Polliangue, and the home (private) was later purchased by his son-in-law, A. D. Smith. It is now (1978) the home of Mrs. Mable Smith, daughter of A. D. Smith.

Six square columns line the gallery, and the front door boasts transom and sidelights. The top halves of the two exterior chimneys are gone now. Exposed, beaded beams may be found in the older section of the home.

Cross Pine street, and drive farther along Chatrian to the second home on the right.

Other Downtown Homes

There are several interesting homes (all private) in downtown Grand Coteau about which very little is known. The first of these (see directions above) has been a Barry family home since the 1870s or early 1880s (and still is, as of 1978). Six square columns line its screened gallery. There are two dormer windows and two exterior chimneys.

A bit farther down Chatrian Street, on the right, is the old Castille-Chatrian home, whose builder and date of construction are unknown. Six columns line the gallery, and there are two dormer windows and two exterior chimneys. Two transomed doors flank the main entrance, with its transom and sidelights. The home's old wooden cistern remains.

Turn left on Cherry Street, drive to Main, turn left and drive half a block to the beautiful "Cajun cabin" (on the left). This is a classic example of the one-front-room version of the Creole-Caribbean cottages that are now com-

monly called "Cajun cabins." It was probably built prior to 1850, and it is believed that it was owned for a time by Nathaniel Levy, who kept it as a residence for his two sons who were students at St. Charles College. Two small double doors open onto the tiny gallery, and a two-tier stairway leads from the gallery to the attic. There is one exterior chimney, and board shutters cover the side windows. The home has been considerably expanded to the rear. (The Cajun cabin traditionally has an interior chimney, whether the home is of the one-room or two-room variety. A major exception exists, however, in a roughly triangular region including Marksville, Opelousas, and the upper Teche, where the chimneys are frequently exterior—but this is an English influence.)

Drive farther up Main Street, and cross St. Joseph Street. The first home on the right is an interesting cypress house which was built in 1868 by André Meche. It is now (1978) owned by Mr. and Mrs. William Foraz, and Mr. Foraz is the grandson of the builder. Six columns and a balustrade line the gallery, and a stairway leads from gallery to attic. A rear gallery has unusual wooden arches at each end.

Drive farther up Main to Burleigh, turn right and drive one block to St. Charles Street, turn right again and drive half a block to the Andrus home on the left. Now (1978) owned by Mrs. Odelle Andrus, this home has been in the Andrus family during most of this century, but its builder and date of construction are unknown. Six square columns may be seen along the single gallery, and there are two exterior chimneys. A transom and sidelights adorn the single front entrance.

On the left, just past the Andrus home, facing St. Charles Street and on the near side of Market Street, is a cottage of obviously great age. It has been a rental property for many years, and its builder and date of construction are not known. Its small double door is flanked by two single doors, and four columns line the little gallery.

Drive farther down St. Charles Street, and cross Church Street to enter the parking lot of Sacred Heart Church. Charles Smith, of one of the earliest families of the Grand Coteau area, donated 130 arpents of land for St. Charles Church in 1819. Construction of the church building had begun in 1817, or, in any event, Smith's contract with the builders is dated June 14, 1817. (Smith later received some payment from Bishop Louis William Dubourg, but it is unclear whether the payment was for the buildings, the lands, or both.) The church was dedicated in October of 1820, but Smith had died suddenly the previous year.

The present church, called Sacred Heart, was built in 1879 and dedicated in 1880. The architect was James Freret of New Orleans, and the church is a pleasant frame building of Georgian design. Its interior is memorable, with Belgian altars, statuary, gleaming woodwork, and many paintings (including those of the Mysteries of the Rosary and Stations of the Cross).[32]

From the parking lot of the church, turn right on Church Street, cross Peach Street, and drive to the third home on the left, a small cottage that is shaded by large oaks. Until recently this home was a property of St. Charles College, and its builder and date of construction are unknown. Six square columns line the single gallery, and its doorway features a transom and sidelights. There are two exterior chimneys.

> From the cottage on Church Street, drive 0.5 mile farther out Church Street to a sharp right curve. From the curve, drive straight ahead on the gravel drive that leads around a curve and up a hill to the old Smith-Barry home.

Old Smith-Barry Home

Eight square columns line the single gallery of this large home (private) and a gallery door provides access to each of the three front rooms. Brick steps lead to the center of the gallery, and louvered shutters protect all exterior windows. The home is set on two-foot brick foundations, and two dormer windows may be seen on the end-gabled roof. There are two chimneys, one exterior and one interior, which makes it seem likely that the home was once enlarged. There are three back rooms, and the center one now serves as a dining room.

The home was built in the early 1800s by

The old Smith-Barry home of Grand Coteau was built by the brother of Charles Smith.

Benjamin A. Smith, who had traveled to Grand Coteau from Maryland in 1806 with several brothers. One brother (Charles Smith, whose family donated the lands for the church, convent and college) built a home quite similar to this one and in a direct line with it in 1811, and the Smith-Barry home may well have been built that same year or earlier. (Charles Smith's home burned in 1978.) Rachael J. Smith, Benjamin's son, inherited the home in 1872, and it was purchased several years later by J. C. Barry—grandfather of the present (1978) owner, Mr. J. R. Barry. J. C. Barry's son Robert married the grandniece of Benjamin Smith, so the present owner is a descendant of the first, as well as the second, owners of the home.

> Return via the gravel drive to the asphalt road (the extension of Church Street) and turn left. It is 0.4 mile to the parking lot of the Academy of the Sacred Heart.

Academy of the Sacred Heart

The huge and beautiful main building of the Academy of the Sacred Heart is set in the midst of nine acres of massive oaks, towering pine trees, and formal gardens. The garden immediately in front of the building was created in

1835 by Madame Xavier Murphy, and its many brick-enclosed sections are in a variety of geometric forms. A double row of pines, planted in 1850, leads to the chapel.

Mrs. Charles Smith, who owned a large plantation in the Grand Coteau area, invited the Religious of the Sacred Heart to establish a school here, and she offered to provide land and pay the traveling expenses of the nuns. The first colony of that order in the United States had been established on the East Coast in 1818, and the Academy in Grand Coteau was to be their second establishment. Mother Eugenie Audé and Sister Mary Layton arrived at Mrs. Smith's home in August of 1821, and three weeks later they moved into a large home provided for them by their benefactress. (This original structure of the Academy was destroyed by fire in 1922.) The Academy was founded in October, 1821, and today it is the oldest (in continuous operation) of the 212 Sacred Heart schools around the world.

Mother Audé, who had been a member of the Napoleonic Court before entering the Society of the Sacred Heart in France, was among the first party of these nuns to arrive in the United States, and Sister Layton was the first American postulate received in the order. Mother Xavier

Murphy arrived in Grand Coteau in April of 1822, and she served as superior during the formative years of the school.

The original section of the present building, consisting of the lower two floors of the central third, was constructed by a builder named William Moore, and the first brick was laid on September 30, 1830. This section can be distinguished by its brick pattern, called Flemish Bond, consisting of rows of lengthwise bricks alternating with rows of widthwise bricks. The two lower floors of the east section were added in 1834 by Samuel Young, who had built Chretien Point in 1831. The brick pattern of this section consists of layers of lengthwise bricks, five rows deep, broken by widthwise bricks which may be seen on every sixth row. The galleries of the 1830 section were extended to front the second section as well, and those of the newer section were given wooden columns and balustrades to match the older galleries.

The three-story western third of the building was added around 1845, and the third floors of the central and eastern thirds of the structure were added in the 1870s. It was probably at this later date that the cast-iron columns and balustrades were added to the galleries of all three sections, replacing the wooden embellishments of the older sections.[33] The attached Georgian chapel was added to the west end in 1850, and its pediment rests on four pilasters. The chapel was balanced by the addition in the 1870s of the matching library wing on the east end of the main building. Standing near the library wing is Memorare Hall, built in 1938, which is now connected to the library by an arcade.

Behind the massive Academy stands the old slave quarters built in 1834. (A family of servants had been provided by Mrs. Smith.) This now serves as a faculty residence, and its wings and second floor appear to be later additions. Just west of the quarters and attached to the rear of the Academy is the long brick kitchen wing, built in 1922, which is a near replica of the original. A bit farther west is the huge brick barn, built in 1854–1855. Arched entrances designed to accommodate loaded hay wagons may be seen here and there, and the section which once sheltered horses and carriages now serves as a garage for school busses.

The war years were hard ones for the Academy. Regular classes were largely discontinued, replaced by training in skills formerly practiced by the slaves of the wealthy families whose daughters were students here—cooking, household chores, and even the care and milking of cows—because the wise nuns could see the handwriting on the wall. The school often ran dangerously short of food and supplies, and, though the students and faculty were Southerners, help came on one occasion from Union General Nathaniel Banks. He corresponded with the nuns by courier, shortly after the fall of Opelousas on April 20, 1863, and at the request of the mother superior he sent one hundred pounds of coffee, five barrels of meal, two barrels of flour, a half-chest of tea, a barrel of sugar, and three bags of salt (no doubt confiscated from recently captured Avery Island). Banks' own daughter was a student at the Manhattanville Convent of the Sacred Heart in New York. He also promised, at the request of the superior in Grand Coteau, that he would provide all possible protection to the convent in Natchitoches. His letters may still be found in the Academy archives.

In October of 1866, a violent hemorrhage endangered the life of a young postulate named Mary Wilson, and two physicians pronounced her disease incurable. In December the nuns made a novena to Blessed John Berchmans (a former Jesuit scholastic who was being considered by the Church for canonization) in behalf of the young girl, but she grew worse and even received Extreme Unction (the last rites of the Roman Catholic Church). On December 14, as she lay dying, she herself prayed to John Berchmans, and it is said that he appeared to her immediately and that she was cured.[34] The saint appeared to her again when she was writing an account of the miracle to be submitted to Rome. The second appearance occurred as she was praying for assistance to record the events properly, and it is said that the saint assured her that her memory of the details was accurate. The little Academy infirmary where the saint

The many-columned galleries of the old Academy of the Sacred Heart are flanked by Georgian wings that contain chapel and library.

appeared now contains a shrine in his honor, and Mary Wilson's account of his appearances was used in Rome as partial evidence for his eventual canonization. The girl later became a Sister of the Sacred Heart, and her grave may be seen today in the old Academy cemetery.

A massive oak alley, planted in 1840 by Father Nicolas Point, leads west from the Academy to St. Charles College, founded in 1837 by Father Point. The original structures of the college no longer exist. St. Charles, the first Jesuit college in the South, is now a Jesuit seminary. In its cemetery may be found the grave of the son of Union General William T. Sherman, the Reverend Thomas E. Sherman, who was a Jesuit priest.

From the Academy, return via Church Street to Main Street. Turn left on Main, cross Cherry Street, and drive half a block farther on Main to the old Smith-Brinkhaus home (on the right).

Old Smith-Brinkhaus Home

This home (private) was probably built circa 1810–1815, probably by one of the brothers of Robert Burleigh. (The Burleigh family arrived in Grand Coteau in 1798.) The home later entered the Smith family through marriage, and William Brinkhaus became the owner (probably around the turn of the century) when he married Isabella Smith. The Brinkhauses had arrived from Germany in the 1850s, and the home remained in the Brinkhaus family until the 1970s, when it was purchased and restored by Mr. and Mrs. Fred Bandy.

The dwelling was constructed of handhewn cypress beams and timbers, and it is set on two-foot brick foundations. A wooden balustrade and six square columns enclose the gallery, and there is one exterior chimney. Windows with louvered shutters and one transomed doorway complete the facade.

Drive one block farther along Main Street to Bellemin Street (La. 760–2). Turn right on La. 760–2 and drive 0.7 mile to La. 182. Turn left and drive 0.3 mile on 182 to the driveway (on the right) of the old McPherson home. This is a private home, but turn into the driveway to view it, because La. 182 is narrow here and the home is situated in a sharp curve.

OLD McPHERSON HOME

It is believed that this fine old home (private) was built by a McPherson family, but its date of construction is unknown. A later owner was Simon Levi, whose widow removed the second-floor gallery (in 1946 or shortly thereafter) and replaced it by adding an individual balcony on each window of that level. Upper and lower balconies on the rear of the home (which may have taken the form of a pedimented portico) are also gone now. Mr. and Mrs. Charles Bernard restored the home during the period of 1968–1971, and they added first-floor ceiling beams to bolster the sagging floor of the second level. They plan to replace the upper gallery eventually.

Eight slender wooden pillars rise two stories from the remaining gallery to the eave of the end-gabled roof, and the front door is adorned with transom and sidelights. A straight stairway with a handsome newel rises from the central hallway to the second floor, and the old servant stairway still rises from a back room that is now used as a pantry. The wide facings of the mantels and major doorways share an interesting design, and beneath the two mantels may be seen the arched brickwork of the fireplaces. The

The Smith-Brinkhaus home in Grand Coteau.

old kitchen building, once separate, is now attached to the rear of the home.

> From the driveway of the old McPherson home, drive 2.5 miles farther along La. 182 to U.S. 167. Turn right and drive 1.0 mile to an unmarked asphalt road and turn left. The first home on the right (facing U.S. 167 from atop the hill) is the old Breaux-Kidder home.

BREAUX-KIDDER HOME

Four tapered columns and a wooden balustrade line the little gallery of this cypress and *bousillage* cottage (private). The age of the home and its builder are unknown, but it was purchased early in this century by Anistar Breaux. It has been the home of his daughter and son-in-law, J. B. Kidder, for many years. The home was raised a bit in recent years, and it is now set on modern foundations. There is one exterior chimney.

> From the Breaux-Kidder home, drive 0.7 mile farther along the unmarked road (crossing a railroad track), and turn left on a lane that leads 0.6 mile through a field to the old home called L'Isle Carencro. L'Isle Carencro and the lane that leads to it are private, and this information is provided only for the purpose of documenting the existence and location of the home.

L'ISLE CARENCRO

This handsome old one-and-one-half-story cottage (private) was built around 1800 by David Guidry, who died in 1821, and it was occupied during the years of the War Between the States by his grandson, Thelismar Guidry.[35] It was abandoned some years later, after several changes in ownership, and it stood neglected until 1970 when it was inherited and restored by Dr. and Mrs. David Edmonds. (Mrs. Edmonds is a matrilineal descendant of Thelismar Guidry.)

Two doors and four high windows (not original) open onto the single gallery, which is enclosed by a wooden balustrade. Six half-brick-half-wood columns support the end-gabled roof, and portions of the facade have been sheathed in brick. The home rests on twelve-by-twelve pegged cypress beams, and inside may still be seen the original beaded ceiling boards and ceiling beams. The original mantel still graces the exterior chimney, and the old herb cellar may still be found beneath the stairway. The stairs descend from bedrooms to the dining room, now enclosed, which was once a loggia that opened on the rear of the home. The old interior doors, built of vertical boards, were used as operating tables when Thelismar Guidry's home was pressed into service as a field hospital during the Battle of Bayou Bourbeaux, and it is said that the owner's cotton bales were torn apart to provide improvised bedding for the wounded.

After the Battle of Vermilionville in 1863, some forty thousand Union troops were encamped between Bayous Carencro and Bourbeaux from mid-October through the first of November, but Union General Banks ordered most of the force to return to Morgan City on November 1. He left four thousand men on the Carencro and some two thousand to guard Bayou Bourbeaux. Just before the battle, Lt. Colonel Theodore Beuhler led two hundred Union troops to scout the area for Confederates, but his entire party was captured without a struggle. (Though he had been overwhelmingly outnumbered, Beuhler drew severe criticism in Northern newspapers for surrendering peacefully.) Some four thousand Confederate cavalrymen then fell on the Union forces at Bayou Bourbeaux about noon on November 3, and one thousand infantrymen quickly moved up on the Yankees' weak right flank. The Union army was routed and might have been captured or massacred at the Bayou Bourbeaux Bridge if the Confederates had pursued them. Dr. James B. Hunter of an Indiana regiment and Doctors Slaughter and Rex of other Union regiments worked feverishly in the Guidry home throughout the afternoon and night to save the lives of the wounded. Confederates and Yankees were later buried together nearby in communal graves.[36]

After the war, the home served for several years as the stagecoach stop between Lafayette and Opelousas. The Guidrys provided food for the travelers and perhaps changes of horses for the stagecoaches.

Return by the dirt road from L'Isle Carencro to the asphalt road, turn right, and drive 0.8 mile to U.S. 167. Turn right and drive 4.1 miles on 167 to the Hector Connolly Road. Turn left and drive 2.6 miles to the Voohries Road. Turn right, and it is 0.1 mile on the Voohries Road to the home called Beaubassin.

LAFAYETTE

One of the first settlers of the Lafayette region was Louis Pierre Arceneaux, the prototype of Longfellow's Gabriel in the story of *Evangeline*. In 1787 Arceneaux settled in the Beaubassin area, near Carencro and now the extreme northern section of Lafayette. In 1795, André Martin settled near what is today the heart of Lafayette, while Marin and Jean Mouton joined Arceneaux near Carencro. Marin and Jean were the sons of Salvador Mouton, an early plantation owner of St. James Parish.

The Mouton family was to play a large part in the history of Lafayette. Jean donated the land for the church and courthouse when the town was laid out in 1825. It was incorporated in 1836 and given the name Vermilionville, for the town is situated on the Vermilion River. The name was changed to Lafayette in 1881. Alexandre Mouton served as the ninth governor—the first Democratic governor—of Louisiana, and his old home now houses the Lafayette Museum. The governor's son Alfred was a Confederate general, and he was chief of staff under General Dick Taylor who opposed Banks in the Bayou Country and Red River campaigns.

Beaubassin

According to age-old local tradition, Louis Pierre Arceneaux ("Gabriel") was the long-lost lover of Emmeline Labiche ("Evangeline") in Henry Wadsworth Longfellow's tragic story, based on the mass exile of the Acadians from present-day Nova Scotia. Arceneaux was from

This picturesque cottage was built by Louis Arceneaux, the prototype of Longfellow's Gabriel.

the area of Acadia called Beaubassin, so that is what he named this farm. He purchased his land from the Attakapas Indians, and he built this home (private) sometime before his death in 1793 (at the age of 62).[37] The home was inherited by Arceneaux's son Louis, and it was later occupied by Louis's daughter Cidalise and her husband, Joseph Mouton (son of Jean Mouton). There followed several changes in ownership, but Beaubassin was brought back into its original family when it was purchased in 1961 by Dr. and Mrs. Thomas J. Arceneaux.

The old one-and-one-half-story home of weatherboarded *bousillage* stands about two feet off the ground on brick foundations, and six slender columns line its single gallery. There are two enclosed end chimneys, with a gallery stairway leading to the attic. Two board front doors, both double, open onto the gallery. A kitchen-dining room wing, separate, is now attached to the center of the home's rear, and a small rear gallery may be seen on one side. Board shutters protect the windows on the sides of the home.

Drive 3.0 miles farther along Voohries Road (which becomes Moss Street—ignore the intersecting roads that will attempt to confuse you as you negotiate two severe "S" curves) to Sidney Martin Street. Turn right and drive 0.2 mile to the old Martin home.

Old Martin Home

This two-and-one-half story raised cottage (private) was probably constructed in the late 1700s or very early 1800s by either a Mouton or a Martin. It was purchased by Sidney Martin in 1918, and it was restored in 1976 by Mr. and Mrs. Norman Smallwood.[38]

Five brick pillars support the upper gallery, which is lined with five smaller, tapered columns and a sturdy balustrade. Three front doors on each level lead to the six front rooms, and there are two back rooms on each floor. The lower floor is constructed of plastered brick, and the upper levels consist of pegged cypress and *bousillage*, with cypress shingles on the exterior walls. The old kitchen has been attached to the rear of the home. Two interior chimneys may be seen on the tin roof, serving six fireplaces. A

delightful curving stairway, steep and said to have been carved in only two pieces from a single log, leads to the attic.

Return via Sidney Martin Street to Moss Street, turn right, and drive 1.4 miles to Alexander Street. Turn left and drive 1.5 miles to Alexander's dead end at Teurlings Street. Turn right and drive 0.8 mile to East Pine Street. Turn left on Pine and drive 0.2 mile to Anita Street. Turn right on Anita, drive to Blanchet Drive, turn right, and drive one block to the old Andrus home (on the left).

Joseph Andrus Home

This beautiful home (private) stood originally in Opelousas, where it was constructed by Joseph Andrus circa 1803—the year of his marriage. It was moved and restored in 1977 by architect Robert E. Smith. Eight colonettes line the gallery of the Andrus home, and there are three paneled, transomed doors. The gallery wall boasts elaborate paneling and wainscoting. The gallery's beaded ceiling boards are extremely wide (perhaps eighteen to twenty inches), and the old beaded beams remain (the two end beams are set diagonally).

This is a Federal style home with the typical Creole floorplan—the large central room flanked by two smaller rooms on the front, and two minor rooms flanking a central loggia (now enclosed with glass) on the rear. The old stair-

The Joseph Andrus home, recently moved from Opelousas, boasts fine paneling and exceptional faux-marbre *woodwork.*

way leads from loggia to attic. The woodwork is of tulip poplar, though the floor of the lower level and an occasional beam are of cypress. The walls of the lower floor are insulated with *bousillage*. Inside may be seen the tulip poplar ceiling boards and beams and the raised-panel walnut doors. One chimney serves two fireplaces, and at least five colors are evident in the unusually elaborate *faux-marbre* mantels, wainscoting, and baseboards. One could consider himself distinguished if his home contained woodwork decorated in the old art of *faux marbre* (wood painted to resemble marble), but Joseph Andrus went a step farther—his woodwork resembles marble inlaid with other varieties of marble.

> Return via Blanchet, Anita, and East Pine streets to Teurlings Street, turn left, and drive 0.5 mile on Teurlings to Porter Lane. Turn left on Porter and drive 0.1 mile to the home (on the left) at 103 Porter Lane.

Old Guilbeau Home

. Believed to have been constructed around 1810 by Jean Guilbeau, this home (private) stood west of Carencro on Carencro Bayou until 1975, when it was moved to its present location and restored by Mrs. Gertrude Trahan.[39] She was assisted by restoration architect Robert E. Smith.

The Charles Mouton home, built in 1848, is a fine example of the end-gabled Creole raised cottage.

Eight colonettes line the 50-foot gallery of the end-gabled cottage, which is set three or four feet off the ground on brick foundations. The bays between the foundations are ornamented with latticework. A stairway from the left end of the long gallery leads to the attic beneath the tin roof. The home was built of *bousillage* and pegged cypress, and its beams, doors, and other woodwork are beaded. Two small back rooms flank a loggia which is now enclosed with glass.

Behind the home stands a small cottage built about 1840 in Washington, Louisiana, which was also moved here and restored by Mrs. Trahan.

> From 103 Porter Lane, drive half a block farther on Porter to St. Marguerite Street. Turn right and drive two blocks to Carmel Drive (La. 94). Turn right on Carmel and drive 0.9 mile to Louisiana Avenue. Turn left and drive 0.3 mile on Louisiana to Simco. Turn right on Simco and drive 0.5 mile to Sterling Street. Turn right on Sterling and drive 0.1 mile to the home on the right numbered 338 North Sterling.

Charles Mouton Home

This handsome raised cottage (private) is set in the midst of pines and magnolias on a large lawn, and it was built in 1848 by Lt. Governor Charles Homer Mouton. Union General Banks made the Mouton home his Lafayette headquarters when his army passed through the town of Vermilionville in 1863.

Dr. Sterling Mudd occupied the home for a time after the war. He was the nephew of Dr. Samuel A. Mudd, who was convicted for conspiracy when he set the broken leg of John Wilkes Booth. Booth's leg had been broken in his jump to the stage from Lincoln's box seat, but the assassin had miraculously escaped the theater. Though Dr. Mudd claimed at his trial that he had not known the circumstances of the injury when he treated Booth, and though most doctors would agree that treatment should have been performed under any circumstances, the doctor was sentenced to life in prison. He was pardoned four years later by President Andrew Johnson. The home was later purchased and restored by Mayor and Mrs. Kenneth Bowen.

A double door above and a single door below,

both with transoms and sidelights, open from the center of the home onto the galleries, and the central doorway on each floor is flanked by two transomed French doors. Six square brick columns support the upper gallery, on which may be seen six square wooden columns and a wooden balustrade. The home was built of brick, pegged cypress, and *bousillage*, and there is an enclosed chimney on each end.

From the old Mouton home, drive two blocks farther along Sterling to Goldman Street, turn left, and drive one-half block to the old home (on the left) at 518 Goldman. This cottage (private), built circa 1850 in Breaux Bridge, was moved here and restored in the 1970s by Mrs. Gertrude Trahan. Drive one-half block farther on Goldman to Elizabeth Street, turn left on Elizabeth, and drive two blocks to Mudd Street. Turn right on Mudd and drive two blocks to the Southwest Evangeline Thruway. Turn left on the thruway and drive 1.2 miles to Pinhook Road. Turn right on Pinhook and drive 1.3 miles to the large home (on the right) at 1340 Pinhook Road.

Old Acadian Inn

Built in the late 1700s or very early 1800s, this building—commonly called the Old Acadian Inn—has served as a plantation home and a hotel (one of Lafayette's first), and it now (1978) houses a restaurant and lounge called Judge Roy Bean's. There was a steamboat landing nearby, on the Vermilion River, during the days when the old structure was an inn.

Eight two-story square columns line the upper and lower galleries, which are enclosed by wooden balustrades. An octagonal *garçonnière*, which today contains a small lounge, was added in the 1950s and attached to the main

This fine old inn now houses a restaurant and lounge in downtown Lafayette.

structure by an enclosed passageway. One door with transom and sidelights opens onto the center of the lower gallery, and two doors serve the upper gallery. An enclosed chimney may be seen on each end of the gabled, shingled roof. The old exposed, beaded beams may be seen in the original rooms of the building, which consisted of two front rooms and two minor rear rooms on each floor. The old rear stairway still exists, though the rear gallery it served is now part of the large back rooms that have been added through the years.

Drive one-half block farther on Pinhook Road to Bendel Road, turn right on Bendel, and drive to South College Road. Turn left on South College and drive 0.2 mile to Girard Park Drive, which leads through Girard Park.

Battle of Vermilionville

Retreating from Union General Nathaniel Banks's advancing army after the Confederate victory at Irish Bend, General Dick Taylor passed through Lafayette on April 17, 1863. His wagons were straggling, and Union troops came into view just as the wagons were crossing the Vermilion River at the point that is now Girard Park. The Yankees later claimed two captured wagons, but most crossed safely and the Confederates burned the bridge. The 1st Company of the 18th Louisiana Regiment, under the command of General Alfred Mouton, deployed along the west bank of the river and kept the Union force penned down for hours, unable to install a pontoon bridge, until the wagons were far away and safe.[40]

Banks met Taylor and Mouton again in the Red River Campaign, and his advance on Shreveport was finally crushed by Taylor at the Battles of Pleasant Hill and Mansfield. Mouton died at Mansfield.

From Girard Park, drive farther along Girard Park Drive (it becomes Taft Street) to University Avenue. Turn left and drive to the cottage (on the right) at 704 West University (just beyond the St. Landry Street intersection, across from Sears).

Beaubassin Cottage

The walls of this cottage (private) are of mud and moss covered with weatherboards. Four colonettes line the gallery, and the balustrade is of a crossed-diamond design. A steep stairway leads to the attic from the gallery, which is served by two front doors. The little building, constructed about 1836, is said to have served as a schoolhouse for a time, and it originally stood in the Beaubassin area of north Lafayette.

Drive one block farther on West University to West Convent, turn right, and round the curve on Convent to St. John Street. Turn left on St. John and drive one block to St. John's Cathedral.

St. John's Oak and Cemetery

On the grounds of the impressive St. John's Cathedral (built in 1916) is the massive St. John Oak, a member of the Louisiana Live Oak Society. Here also, in the church cemetery, are the graves of two Confederate generals, Alfred Mouton and Franklin Gardner. Also buried here is Cidalise Arceneaux, the daughter of Louis Pierre Arceneaux (the Gabriel of Longfellow's *Evangeline*), whose old home still stands nearby.

From the cathedral, drive one block farther on St. John Street to Vermilion Street. Turn right on Vermilion and drive two blocks to Lafayette Street. Turn right on Lafayette and drive one and one-half blocks to the old Hebert house (on the right) at 1016 Lafayette Street.

Old Hebert Home

Four square columns (now half wood and half

cinder block) line the gallery that fronts the original portion of this cottage (private). The old chimney may be seen in the center of that original section. It is believed that the home was built in the 1820s, and it was acquired about 1840 by Ursin Hebert, Sr. It was inherited in the 1880s by Ursin Jr., who added the southern third of the structure around the turn of the century. Two doors with transoms lead from the gallery to the original rooms, where the original exposed beams may still be seen.

Drive one block farther along Lafayette Street to the Lafayette Museum (on the right) at 1122 Lafayette.

Lafayette Museum

The Lafayette Museum is housed in the fine old building that was once the home of Governor Alexandre Mouton. The first floor, along with the *briquette-entre-poteau* kitchen which still stands in the rear, was built by the governor's father, Jean Mouton, perhaps as early as the first decade of the 1800s. Alexandre was born in 1804 in his father's older home on Bayou Carencro. He attended Georgetown before "reading law" in the office of Judge Edward Simon in St. Martinville. He was elected to the state legislature in 1829 (he served twice as speaker of the house), and he was selected in 1837 to complete the unexpired term of U.S. Senator Alexander Porter. He resigned from the Senate in 1842 to run for governor, and he was the first Democrat ever elected to that post. Mouton presided at the state convention in Baton Rouge, which on January 26, 1861, voted Louisiana out of the Union. Mouton had favored secession, and his son Alfred became a Confederate general and died in the Battle of Mansfield in Northwest Louisiana.

The old Jean Mouton home was purchased in 1836 by Louisiana Chief Justice Cornelius Voohries. In 1849 it was purchased by William G. Mills, who added the second floor, the attic, and the cupola. The museum was established in 1954, and admission is free. It is open from 9:00 a.m. to noon and from 2:00 p.m. to 5:00 p.m. Tuesday through Saturday, and from 3:00 to 5:00 on Sunday afternoons.

The Lafayette Museum is housed in the fine old home of Governor Alexandre Mouton.

This two-and-one-half-story weatherboarded building is fronted by two galleries and six stately square columns. An octagonal cupola, open but sheltered, with a protective railing, can be seen atop the gable roof. The walkway that leads to the home is lined with sweet olive and dwarf magnolias. In the hallway are an ornate plaster medallion, maps of Louisiana dated 1820 to 1828, and a lithograph of Alexandre Mouton.

The museum is filled with historic weapons, tools, portraits, and fine antique furniture, but several items bear specific mention—a quilt made by Abraham Lincoln's mother, a hand-woven bedspread and pillow case dating to 1613, an 1859 copy of *Le Pionnier de l'Assomption* from Napoleonville, and an 1864 copy printed on wallpaper of *Le Courrier des Opelousas*. The third floor is devoted to display rooms which feature the costumes of the kings and queens of Lafayette's two Mardi Gras krewes, the Order of Troubadours and the Southwest Louisiana Mardi Gras Association.

Drive half a block farther on Lafayette Street to Barry Street. Turn left and drive to Lee Avenue. Turn left and drive one block to the intersection of Lee and Jefferson streets. In front of the Lafayette City Hall stands the statue of Confederate General Alfred Mouton.

Continue along Lee Avenue and drive about five blocks from the statue to Vermilion Street. Turn left and drive one block to the San Souci Bookstore (on the right) at 219 East Vermilion.

San Souci Bookstore

It is not known when this shotgun style building was constructed, but by 1866 it was being used as the Vermilionville Post Office, with John H. Chargois serving as postmaster. Since then it has been a print shop, a pecan store, a tin shop, a shoe shop and an antiques store. It now (1978) houses the San Souci Bookstore, which offers a large selection of books on Louisiana and the South. The building is roofed in tin, and the weatherboards are painted rust red. The large bay windows are not original.

Drive one and one-half blocks farther on Vermilion to Jefferson Street, turn right, and drive two blocks to Garfield. Turn right and drive 0.2 mile on Garfield to Johnston Street. Turn right on Johnston and drive 4.7 miles to Ridge Road (La. 342). Turn right and drive 1.7 miles to Mouton Road. Turn left on Mouton and drive 0.4 mile to the Alleman Center Road, which leads 0.3 mile to the Acadian Village and Tropical Gardens.

Acadian Village

The delightful Acadian Village is a complex of five historic homes moved here from various Cajun Country locations, plus certain other buildings constructed in the time-honored style of the earliest settlers here, that together depict life in an early nineteenth century bayouside village. Brick pathways follow Bayou Alleman past the old homes, through the Around-the-World Tropical Gardens, and past (summers only) craftsmen practicing pioneer skills.

A visitor first encounters the Trading Post, built here of *briquette-entre-poteau* construction, where ladies in Acadian costumes sell books on the Acadians, Cajun record albums, and many items of Acadian arts and crafts made at the Alleman Center (for the retarded) and at senior citizens homes throughout Lafayette Parish. The Alleman Center, which provides training and livelihood for the retarded, opened in 1976 on the 32-acre site that was donated for this purpose in 1972 by Mr. and Mrs. E. L. Alleman.

The Thibodeaux house, moved here from Breaux Bridge, was built circa 1800 by Narcisse Thibodeaux, and it is said to be haunted by Oray Thibodeaux, third son of Narcisse. It was built of *bousillage* and pegged cypress, raised about two feet above the ground on huge cypress blocks. Eight posts line the single gallery, and a stairway leads from gallery to attic. A central chimney serves the two main rooms of the home, and the old cistern may still be seen in the rear. Interior walls are covered with plaster made of lime and deer hair.

Next door stands the old LeBlanc home from Youngsville, where its original room and attic were built in the 1820s. The home was enlarged in the 1850s, and it was the birthplace in 1894 of the "Hadacol King," Louisiana's colorful State

Above: *Three of the historic structures that now stand at Acadian Village in Lafayette are (left to right) the old cottage from St. John Street in Lafayette, built about 1840; the boyhood home of Hadacol King Dudley LeBlanc, built in Youngsville in the 1820s; and the old Thibodeaux house from Breaux Bridge, built about 1800.*

Below: *Other interesting buildings at Acadian Village are (left to right) the Dorsene Castille home from Breaux Bridge, built in 1830; a replica of a church typical of those found along the bayous in the mid-1800s; and the old servants quarters of Billeaud Plantation near Broussard.*

Senator Dudley J. LeBlanc, who concocted the patent medicine called Hadacol that is still in use today. The top singing stars and film stars of the day joined LeBlanc in the roving promotional show called the Hadacol Caravan, and it was on one such junket through South Louisiana that Hank Williams wrote his most famous song, "Jambalaya." Inside the old cottage are displayed photos of LeBlanc and several of his personal possessions.

Just beyond the LeBlanc home is another small cottage, moved here from St. John Street in Lafayette where it had been constructed around 1840 of cypress timbers from an earlier building. Four cypress columns line its little gallery, and the wall between its two main rooms has been removed to provide ample space for the display of vintage spinning and weaving paraphernalia.

Across Bayou Alleman, accessible by a rustic footbridge, stands the old house-servants' quarters from Billeaud Plantation near Broussard. The steps to the gallery and the two front doors are off-center, and five colonettes line the gallery. The old building now contains a woodworking shop. Next door to the Billeaud slave house stands the brick village church, a replica of the typical churches that could have been found in small bayou towns in the 1850s. Next to the church is the old Castille home, built about 1830 in Breaux Bridge by Dorsene Castille. Interior chimneys are placed at the ends of the gabled roof, and board shutters with their old strap hinges may be seen on the side windows. Six colonettes and a balustrade line the single gallery, and a stairway provides gallery access to the sleeping quarters in the attic.

Adjacent to the village is the Around-the-World Tropical Gardens, where three huge greenhouses and several outside areas provide visitors with a look at the flowers and foliage of the major tropical regions of the world—including the Pacific Islands, Africa, Asia, Latin America, and the Gulf Coast. Acadian Village is open daily, 9:30 a.m. to 5:30 p.m. Memorial Day through Labor Day and 10:00 a.m. to 5:00 p.m. during the remainder of the year. Large tour groups should call (318) 981–2364 for arrangements.

From Acadian Village, return via Alleman Road and Mouton Road to Ridge Road (La. 342). Turn right and drive 1.7 miles to Johnston Street (U.S. 167) and turn right. Drive 14.7 miles south on U.S. 167 to the Highway 14 Bypass in Abbeville. Turn left on the Bypass (Veterans Memorial Drive), and drive 1.6 miles (passing the Abbeville Museum and Information Center) to Lafitte Road. Turn right and drive 1.7 miles on Lafitte Road (which becomes Young's Switch) to Jacqulyn Street. Turn right on Jacqulyn and drive 1.5 miles to State Street (Highway 82). Turn left on State Street and drive 0.3 mile to Orange Street. Turn right on Orange and drive 0.6 mile to its dead end, from which a narrow drive (on the right) leads to the Lillywood Plantation home. This home and the driveway that leads to it are private, and this information is provided only for the purpose of documenting the existence and location of the home.

ABBEVILLE AREA

The first sizable community in Vermilion Parish was Perry (or Perry's Bridge), located on Vermilion Bayou just south of Abbeville. The village had grown up around a bridge built by Robert Perry, and that town was named parish seat when Vermilion was carved out of Lafayette Parish in 1844. A Capuchin priest named Father Antoine Megret arrived in 1842, and Robert Perry offered him land for a church near Perry. The land was subject to flooding, however, so Father Megret opted for a tract belonging to Joseph LeBlanc, located north of Perry on a bluff. The priest laid out a town on his acreage in 1843, with two public squares that still exist, and he first named the village La Chapelle. However, Father Megret had been born near Abbeville, France, and the name of his town was soon changed to Abbeville (meaning "Town of the Priest").[41] After much squabbling and two contested referendums, Abbeville was named parish seat in 1855. Father Megret had died of yellow fever in 1853.[42]

Lillywood

Lillywood (private) was built on Vermilion Bayou by Robert Perry in the early 1840s, only a few feet downstream from the toll bridge he had constructed shortly before. Just across the bayou from the home is the village of Perry, which was first named Perry's Bridge. Lillywood was purchased about 1900 by Alcee and B. L. LeBlanc, sons of Joseph LeBlanc (first owner of the land where the city of Abbeville now stands). The home is now (1978) occupied by Christopher LeBlanc, the fifth generation of the family to live here.

Lillywood is two rooms wide, two rooms deep, and two stories high, surmounted by a hipped roof. This house type seems to have originated in the Tidewater region of Virginia, and it "migrated" to Louisiana after 1803. The Louisiana version usually has crossing hallways (that separate the four rooms of each level) and double galleries (on one, two, or four sides of the home). Lillywood, however, has no halls, and its one-story gallery (which wraps around the front and bayou side) was added by the LeBlanc family in the 1920s. Robert Perry had planned imposing galleries for his home, but he died while construction was in progress, and the plans were modified by his widow.

The main entrance, on the viewer's right side of the home, features double doors with pilasters, transom, and sidelights. The ceiling is twelve feet high, and the doorways and double-hung windows throughout the home are extremely high and handsome, ornamented (even the minor doors) with Greek Revival fac-

Lillywood, near Abbeville in the village of Perry, was built by the founder of Abbeville's rival town.

ings. The original mantels, like all the woodwork of Lillywood, are remarkably well preserved, and the home's eight fireplaces are served by two chimneys. The original two-tier stairway rises from a front room. The old servants stairway may still be seen in a rear room.

The front room on the bayou side of the home is the old master bedroom, and its ornate half tester bed has been in the family for many years. A beautifully faced passageway, high and wide, leads from the bedroom to the back room of the bayou side, and both of these rooms have doorways opening onto the gallery that overlooks the bayou. The small building which contains the kitchen and old dining room is attached by a breezeway to the back of the home, and the building's small gallery faces the bayou.

From the driveway of Lillywood, drive less than 0.1 mile back up Orange Street to an unmarked road that leads (left) 0.2 mile to Highway 82. Turn left on 82 and drive 1.3 miles south (through Perry) to the old Stansbury-Schriefer home (on the right), shaded by a massive live oak that stands between the highway and the home.

The old Stansbury-Schriefer home was completed in 1830.

Stansbury-Schriefer Home

Four well-tapered, brick Doric columns, once plastered and now painted white, line the single gallery of this cottage (private). One of the columns, though sturdy, is leaning slightly, and it is said that it has been leaning since the famous hurricane of August, 1856, which destroyed the huge resort hotel on Last Island. The single doorway boasts transom and sidelights, and the old beaded lintel and beams may still be seen on the gallery (though the beams inside the home have been hidden by modern ceiling tiles).

The home was renovated in 1915, and the long dormer above the gallery was added at that time. The *bousillage* was removed from the walls throughout the home, and the walls were resealed with pine. The old gallery stairway was replaced by an interior stair, and a rear wing was created by moving and attaching another old structure which stood nearby. The old cypress floors remain in some of the rooms, as do three of the original, beaded interior doors.

The home was built by the Stansbury brothers, Albert and Summerfield, who had arrived from Baltimore in 1828. They cut their timber that year for curing, and they completed the home in 1830. It was purchased in 1915 by Wesley Schriefer, and it is still (1978) occupied by his son Victor, who was a youngster when his family moved here.

The magnificent, gnarled live oak in the front yard was already spectacular when the Stansburys built the home in 1830. In fact, before seeing the tree they had planned to build a mile or two farther east, on the bayou. The oak must be very old indeed, because (though the fertile soil here is very shallow) it is as large as many of the 300-year-old trees that line the Mississippi. Union soldiers smashed the Stansbury family rifles over the great roots during the war, and Victor Schriefer recalls scores of cattle hanging from the giant limbs at slaughter time.

Southwest Louisiana

The old homes of Southwest Louisiana are rather scattered, so these directions will no longer be given from home to home in the form of a continuous tour. Rather, the directions will be given to each home individually, from Interstate 10.

From Interstate 10 (west of Lafayette and east of Crowley), exit north on Highway 35. From the interstate it is 6.8 miles north to Heritage Farm Village in the town of Branch.

HERITAGE FARM VILLAGE

Heritage Farm Village is a pleasant complex of vintage structures whose focal point is the old Beau family home, moved some five miles from its original location in 1975 and restored by Mr. and Mrs. Gary Frugé. The cabin was built circa 1856 and was the home of a small farmer. Two front doors open onto the single gallery, and steps lead from the gallery to the attic. There was an enclosed chimney on at least one end of the building, but it is gone now. The original home consisted of two front and two rear rooms, but there is now a rear addition.

The Village consists of the home, an old general store and post office, a millinery shop, print shop, and barbershop—all with their appropriate paraphernalia. Also of interest is a sizeable collection of vintage automobiles, including a German Horch said to have belonged to Hitler's mistress. Heritage Farm Village is open for tours, and tickets may be acquired at the adjacent restaurant. Hours are 9:00 a.m. to 5:00 p.m. daily in winter and 9:00 a.m. to 6:00 p.m. daily in summer.

From Interstate 10 in Crowley, exit south on La. 13 (North Parkerson Street) and drive 1.9 miles south (skirting the courthouse) to East Second Street. Turn left on East Second and drive 0.5 mile to South Eastern Avenue (La. 13). Turn right and drive 3.2 miles to La. 3007 (Primeaux Road). Turn right on La. 3007 and drive 2.5 miles to a gravel drive that leads left to the Blue Rose Museum.

BLUE ROSE MUSEUM

This fine old cottage was built circa 1848 near Youngsville, Louisiana, by Olivier Blanchet, and it was moved here and restored in 1964 by Mr. and Mrs. Salmon Lusk Wright, Jr. The land on which it is now situated was homesteaded in 1890 by S. L. Wright, Sr., who developed the world's finest variety of seed rice (called the Blue Rose variety) here in 1912.

Six square columns line the single gallery of the old Blanchet home, which now houses the Blue Rose Museum. A sturdy wooden balustrade leads along the gallery and its center

The fine plantation house that now contains the Blue Rose Museum was built about 1848 near Youngsville.

stairway, and there are gallery gates at the head of the steps. Four windows with louvered shutters flank the great double doorway with its transom and sidelights. The home is set some four feet above the ground on brick foundations. The two end, interior chimneys are now gone. The home was constructed of Louisiana cypress, handmade brick, and *bousillage*.

Heavy and handsome cypress paneling, an unusual feature, covers the gallery wall, and it may also be seen on the interior walls of every first-floor room. A great hallway leads from the front doors to the double back doors (which now provide access to a two-story rear addition). The home's two wooden mantels are original, and the original stairway (with a slight modification at the base) ascends from the hallway. The paneling, since covered with many coats of white paint, was given *faux-bois* ornamentation in 1880, and that work has been uncovered on one bedroom door.

The original four rooms and hallway downstairs and large room upstairs and all of the rooms of the rear addition today house interesting collections of family antiques, china, crystal, silver, dolls, vintage shoes, family portraits, spoons, toys, and heirlooms. Of particular interest are a rocking chair original to the home, a collection of the famous Vargas wax Negro dolls, and a delightful Venetian glass chandelier. The Blue Rose Museum is open 9:30 a.m. to 5:00 p.m. Monday through Friday. It is closed every weekend of the year and every day during January and February, except by appointment. Call (318) 783–3096.

From Interstate 10 in Crowley, exit south on La. 13 (North Parkerson Street) and drive 0.4 mile south to Lake Street. Turn right on Lake Street, and cross Broadacres Street. The second house on the left is the old Andrus home.

OLD ANDRUS HOME

A handsome cast-iron fence surrounds the old Andrus Home, which stands four feet above the ground on brick foundations. Six square beaded columns line the single gallery, and the old beaded balustrade, with gates, lines the gallery and the center stairway. A double front door with transom and sidelights opens onto the center of the gallery, there are two front windows, and French doors open on the viewer's left end of the gallery. The chimneys are gone now, and wooden shingles cover the end-gabled roof.

The cottage was built in Branch, Louisiana, by Joseph Elah Andrus, Jr., in 1839. It was moved to Crowley and restored in 1970 by Mr. and Mrs. Salmon L. Wright, Jr., and it is open for tours by individuals by appointment only, 10:00 a.m. to 4:00 p.m. on weekdays from March 1 through September 1. Groups of twenty or more are welcome all year round, on weekdays, by appointment. Call (318) 783–3096, or inquire at the Blue Rose Museum.

From Interstate 10 (west of Crowley and east of Jennings), exit south on La. 91. Drive 3.6 miles south on La. 91 to the U.S. 90 intersection in the town of Estherwood. Turn left on U.S. 90 and drive two blocks to LeBlanc Street. Turn left on LeBlanc, and drive one block to Estherwood Manor (on the left).

ESTHERWOOD MANOR

The older portion of Estherwood Manor (private) may have been constructed as early as 1840, and it is an end-gabled structure, one room deep, two rooms wide, and two stories high. Six square, two-story columns rise from the gallery to support the gallery's shed roof, and on the upper level beneath the shed roof is a handsome wooden balcony. It is likely that the balcony and gallery are original, though the gallery has been extended on one end and now terminates partway down that side of the home.

The windows are protected by louvered shutters, and the front door boasts sidelights with stained-glass panes. Behind the front rooms, in this older section, were either rear galleries or minor rear rooms, and the old stairway still exists in that area. These are now large rooms, however, because the galleries or small rooms have been enclosed and greatly expanded. A great cross-shaped extension has been added, bit by bit through the years, to the rear of the old home, and the entire structure now contains some twenty rooms. The older section rests on ten-by-twelve cypress beams, and inside may be seen ceiling beams in an interesting pattern and other woodwork of curly cypress.

The builder of Estherwood Manor is unknown, but previous owners have included Eugene Roy and Ellis Hoffpower. The home was recently purchased and restored by Mr. and Mrs. Gerald M. Martin.

> From Interstate 10 (west of Crowley and east of Lake Charles), take Exit 65 and drive 1.5 miles south on Highway 97 (Roberts Avenue) to the intersection of North Cutting Avenue in Jennings. Turn left on North Cutting (Highway 102) and drive 0.7 mile to Academy Avenue. Turn left and drive 1.4 miles to the old Camp Hamilton Home (on the left) at 2200 East Academy.

CAMP HAMILTON HOME

This old home (private) was moved to Jennings in 1977 and restored in 1978 by Judge Walter Peters. It originally stood in Opelousas, where it had served for many years as the overseer's home of Camp Hamilton Plantation. The old *Poste des Opelousas* had become known as Camp Hamilton by the Americans who arrived after 1803, and the fort had consisted of mud and log structures. Judge Seth Lewis arrived in Opelousas in the 1810s or 1820s and bought land that included the old fort site. He called his

The old Andrus home in Crowley was moved here from Branch.

Estherwood Manor may date to 1840.

new estate Camp Hamilton Plantation. For his own home (long since demolished), the judge simply added to and embellished an old log structure remaining from the fort,[43] and it is possible that his overseer's house had also existed before his arrival (though it bears the signs of English influence). If it was not already standing, then it is likely that it was built quickly, surely no later than 1830. It had been unoccupied for some years prior to its move to Jennings.

Six columns and a wooden balustrade line the single gallery of the end-gabled cottage, and there are four evenly spaced windows with pegged, louvered shutters and their original

The Camp Hamilton home, shown here during restoration, was moved to Jennings from Opelousas.

panes. The large double doors opening onto the center of the gallery are transomed, and they are flanked by two smaller sets of French doors, also transomed. The home is roofed with wooden shingles. Handsome baseboards and chair rails may be seen along the gallery wall and throughout the home. The two old interior fireplaces may still be seen inside, but their chimneys have been removed. The original, beaded ceiling beams remain in the three front rooms. A large rear addition has been attached to the cottage since its arrival in Jennings.

> From Interstate 10 in Iowa, exit south on La. 383. Drive through Iowa on 383 to the intersection of U.S. 90. Turn right and drive 5.4 miles on U.S. 90 to a narrow lane, on the right, that leads to LeBleu. This home and the lane that leads to it are private, and this information is provided only for the purpose of documenting the existence and location of the home.

LeBLEU

The first settler in this area was Martin Camersac LeBleu, from Bordeaux, who arrived via Virginia around 1780. His new home was very nearly the jumping-off place, because just to the west—beginning at the Calcasieu River and stretching westward to the Sabine—was the vast no-man's-land that divided Louisiana from Spanish Texas. A year or two after Martin LeBleu came Charles Sallier, who settled a bit to the west on the large lake that now bears his name—Lake Charles. He married the daughter of Bartholomew LeBleu, Catherine, in 1803. (Some say he was a Spaniard who had changed his name from Carlos Salia,[44] though descendants believe he was a Frenchman from Savoy.)

It was early in the nineteenth century when Arsene LeBleu built his handsome two-story home beside the Old Spanish Trail (U.S. 90), and that is the home (private) that still stands here today (though it stands somewhat shorter in its old age). Six heavy square columns lined the two front galleries, and two exterior chimneys flanked the end-gabled roof. The gallery roof, though parallel in pitch to the home's major roof, was set perhaps a foot lower to accommodate short little windows beneath the eave of the higher roof. Through those windows a person in the attic could see (and perhaps shoot) anyone who might be in the front yard.

The bon vivant Arsene, while his horses and cattle grazed his own 200 acres and the endless open rangeland that surrounded his estate, entertained. It is said that he always kept open house, and that a frequent guest was the swashbuckling though refined pirate, Jean Lafitte. Lake Charles served Lafitte as headquarters, or at least as a hideout, for quite some time, and he would stop over at the LeBleu home when he was traveling the Spanish Trail. His men would be quartered in the large barn that burned in 1923. Arsene gave a right-of-way through his property to the Southern Pacific when the railroad was reaching westward, and the company gave LeBleu a station for the private use of the family. Arsene named his station Chloe for his wife, and the village of Chloe still exists about a half-mile west of the home.

Arsene's son, Confederate Major Joseph C. LeBleu, inherited the home after the war. He had been aide de camp to General M. J. Levert, and he lived in this home until his death in the early 1900s. His wife Leonise was an accomplished horsewoman and marksman, and it is said that she once cornered and killed a panther in her hen roost. On another occasion she provided a meal for two road-weary riders, and she refused their offer of payment. She later found their thank-you note, signed Frank and Jesse James.[45]

So the old home that has seen Jean Lafitte, Jesse James, Confederate heroes, and brave pioneers still stands, but it is deteriorating. Its chimneys and, strangely enough, lower floor are gone, and the second-floor rooms and gallery with roof and attic intact have been lowered onto new brick foundations. The old roofline, with the strange little attic windows, is as it was, and the old cypress columns have simply been cut in half. A front door opens onto the center of the gallery, shaded by fig and redbud trees that have grown huge, and two doors with sidelights flank the central entrance.

From Interstate 10 in Lake Charles, exit onto Lakeshore Drive. Lakeshore follows the lake, first east (past the city tourist information office), then south (past the Lake Charles Civic Center), and then west. Follow Lakeshore (which becomes Shell Beach Drive) to Barbe Street. From Barbe Street, continue west, and the second home on the left is the old Barbe house, at 905 Shell Beach Drive.

OLD BARBE HOUSE

This home (private) occupies the site of the first home of the founder of Lake Charles, Charles Sallier, and the original cabin is still contained within the walls of the present structure. The pirate Jean Lafitte was a frequent visitor in Sallier's two-room cabin, and Sallier often traded him meat and vegetables for wine and tobacco. Sallier may even have acted as the pirate's agent, in disposing of Lafitte's slaves and other contraband.[46] A shell mound, thrown up by Lafitte's men for the placement of cannons, once stood on the lakeshore in front of the Barbe house, but the mound was leveled in the early 1900s.

The Barbe house was constructed in the mid-1800s, and six turned colonettes line each of the two front galleries. A balustrade lines the upper gallery beneath the eave of the gabled roof, whose lines appear to have been changed somewhat through the years. A single door opens onto each gallery, and that of the lower level has a transom and sidelights. The large house is raised about a foot on brick foundations, and an attractive gazebo is attached to the gallery on the viewer's right side of the home.

So ends your tour of Bayou Teche and Southwest Louisiana. *Plantation Homes of the Lafourche Country* and *Plantation Homes of the Teche Country* will be followed in order by *Plantation Homes of the Cotton Country* (North Louisiana), *Plantation Homes of the River Roads*, and *Plantation Homes of the Audubon Country* (Florida Parishes).

Notes

1. Harnett T. Kane, *The Bayous of Louisiana* (New York: William Morrow and Company, 1944), pp. 230, 231.

2. Charles Gilbert Stahls, *Grand Bouquet* (Los Angeles: Watling and Company, 1951), p. 182.

3. Morris Raphael, *The Battle in the Bayou Country* (Detroit, Mich.: Harlo Press, 1975), pp. 88-100.

4. Pat Baldridge, "Bocage Starts New Era on Banks of Bayou Teche," *Baton Rouge State Times,* May 23, 1969, Section B, pp. 5, 6.

5. Much of the historical information on the homes of Franklin was provided by Mrs. Florence Blackburn and by the book by Florence Blackburn and Fay Brown, *Franklin Through the Years* (Franklin, La.: Authors, 1972).

6. Lyle Saxon, *Old Louisiana* (New York: Century Company, 1929), p. 357.

7. "Palfrey Residence Once Home of Governor, Private School," *St. Mary-Franklin Banner-Tribune*, April 28, 1959, Section 2, p. 1.

8. "Franklin Home of First Bank Outside of New Orleans before War," *St. Mary-Franklin Banner-Tribune*, April 28, 1959, Section 3, p. 7.

9. Raphael, *The Battle in the Bayou Country*, pp. 107-117.

10. John M. Caffery (son of Donelson Caffery—Confederate soldier and U.S. Senator), "St. Mary Battleground during Civil War," *St. Mary-Franklin Banner-Tribune*, April 28, 1959, Section 3, pp. 1, 2.

11. Lucile Barbour Holmes, *Oaklawn Manor, Ante-bellum Plantation Home* (Franklin, La.: St. Mary Printers, 1966).

12. Information on Vacherie was provided by Mrs. Clyde Alpha, based on her research of the old courthouse records of St. Mary Parish.

13. I am indebted to Mr. Frank R. Duke for much of the information on the Jeanerette area.

14. Frances Parkinson Keyes, *All This Is Louisiana* (New York: Harper and Brothers, 1950), p. 200.

15. Gilbert C. Din, "Lieutenant Colonel Francisco Bouligny and the Malagueno Settlement at New Iberia," *Louisiana History*, 17 (Spring, 1976), pp. 187-202.

16. I am grateful to Mrs. Virginia Hine for her hospitality and for much of the information concerning the homes and history of New Iberia.

17. Saxon, *Old Louisiana*, pp. 361, 362.

18. As quoted by Marian Page, "The Shadows-on-the-Teche," *Interiors*, 122 (February, 1963), pp. 86-93.

19. Michael Durand, "The Lamperez Home—History Lover's Dream," *Daily Iberian*, Jan. 31, 1971.

20. Gerald J. Delcambre, "Reminder of Romantic Bygone Era," *Baton Rouge Sunday Advocate*, July 2, 1967, p. 3-E.

21. Raphael, *The Battle in the Bayou Country*, p. 55.

22. *Ibid*., p. 137.

23. *Ibid*., p. 143.

24. For information on the St. Martinville area, I am indebted to Mr. James Acres, curator of the Petite Paris Museum, and to Mrs. Leona Martin Guirard. Mrs. Guirard was until recently curator of the Acadian House Museum in the Longfellow-Evangeline Commemorative Area, and she shared much information through conversation as well as through her book, *St. Martinville—The Land of Evangeline in Picture Story* (1950).

25. George W. Cable, *Strange True Stories of Louisiana* (New York: Charles Scribner's Sons, 1889), p. 93.

26. Milton B. Newton, Jr., "Louisiana House Types—A Field Guide," *Melanges*, no. 2 (September 27, 1971), p. 13.

27. Foundation for Historical Louisiana, *Tour des Maisons de l'Acadie* (Baton Rouge, La.: 1973), pp. 17-18.

28. Cable, *Strange True Stories of Louisiana*, pp. 34-120.

29. "Robin Home, Bayou Teche," *Opelousas Daily World*, 250th Opelousas Anniversary Edition, June, 1970, p. 60.

30. I am indebted to Mr. C. Kenneth Deshotel and Judge Joseph A. LaHaye for information and assistance in the Leonville area.

31. Much of the information on the old homes and buildings of Grand Coteau was provided by Mr. C. Kenneth Deshotel and Mrs. Chloe Mills.

32. Jane Olivier, *The Church of St. Charles* (Grand Coteau, La., 1975), pp. 1-4, 17, 18.

33. Academy of the Sacred Heart, National Register of Historic Places—Nomination Form, on file in the office of the Louisiana Division of Archaeology and Historic Preservation, Old Capitol Building, Baton Rouge.

34. Rev. C. J. McNaspy, "The Miracle at Grand Coteau" (undated booklet).

35. Martha Aycock, "Screams of Dying Men Once Filled This House," *Lafayette Daily Advertiser*, April 11, 1976.

36. Information on the Battle of Bayou Bourbeaux was provided by Dr. David Edmonds, based on his research for a forthcoming book on the war in this region.

37. Debbie D'Aquin, "Beaubassin, Old Acadian Home," *Lafayette Daily Advertiser*, August 8, 1976.

38. Eleanor Yount, "Martin Home One of Oldest in Parish," *Lafayette Daily Advertiser*, Sept. 6, 1976.

39. Debbie D'Aquin, "House Untouched by Time," *Lafayette Daily Advertiser*, Oct. 24, 1976, p. 36.

40. Raphael, *The Battle in the Bayou Country*, pp. 145-148.

41. Clare D'Artois Leeper, *Louisinia Places* (Baton Rouge, La.: Legacy Publishing Co., 1976), p. 5.

42. I am indebted to Mrs. Euna Evans for information on the old homes of Vermilion Parish.

43. "Camp Hamilton," *Opelousas Daily World*, 150th St. Landry Anniversary Edition (1955), pp. 7-8. (Contains an account by Mrs. Amelia Watts, granddaughter of Judge Lewis, who visited the Judge's plantation in 1832.)

44. Lyle Saxon (state supervisor, Louisiana Writers Program, Work Projects Administration), *Louisiana, a Guide to the State* (New York: Hastings House, 1941), p. 282.

45. Albert Proctor, "Knitting Is Pastime for Grandma Joe over Sunset Years," *The Progress*, Jan. 28, 1938. (Contains an interview with the widow of Major LeBleu.)

46. Billy McGraw, "Spirit of Lafitte, Maybe Gold, Still Haunts Winding Calcasieu," *Lake Charles American Press*, November 17, 1963.

Index